You Can't fly with a Broken Wing

You Can't Fly with a Broken Wing

Dick Innes

ACTS
COMMUNICATIONS

PO Box 73545 • San Clemente
California • U.S.A. 92673-0119
www.actscom.com/store

Published by ACTS Communications
PO Box 73545
San Clemente, California 92673-0119
U.S.A.

Library of Congress Cataloguing-in-Publication Data

Innes, Dick
You Can't Fly With a Broken Wing:
- ACTS Communications

ISBN 0-9642525-3-8
1. Recovery (Psychology)
2. Healing, Wholeness–Religious aspects–Christianity

Cover art: Dean Clark
Cover photo: Dick Innes
Copy editing: Carol Lacy Pell

Printed in the United States of America

Contents

Introduction

For most of my adult life I ran from love. It was easy for me to *love* where love was not available. That was safe. But where love was available, that was a different story. Love me and I would find or make up an excuse to run—then look for love again—and run again. Consequently, loneliness plagued me much of my life.

I had no idea why I would run from love. Even less did I know that I was afraid to love. In fact, a psychological inventory revealed that I had a hidden terror. On a scale of zero to one hundred, with anything below thirty considered repressed, I scored one! I had no idea where this terror came from, or why I had it, and that it was causing me to run from love.

Because of my fear (terror) I was attracted to and married a woman who, because of her childhood trauma, was also afraid to love. It turned out to be a disastrous relationship for we lived together alone apart—and died a little every day.

All I knew was that I had failed in love. Though successful in my professional life, in my personal life I constantly felt empty and in my love life, lonely. My pain motivated me to get into recovery.

Later—a decade later.

When I met Joy and she began to love me I was overwhelmed with fear and wanted to run—again. But I knew that if I didn't face and overcome my fear now, I would be running from love for the rest of my life.

More recovery needed.

I thank Joy for sticking with me while I worked through and resolved my terror for it was her love that caused me to confront it and get the help I needed to overcome it. This, in turn, made it possible for me to finish this book that I actually started to write several years ago, but knew that I couldn't finish it until I had "lived the last chapter."

This book is not about my fear of loving and the causes behind it (that may come later). It is a book about the healing of the whole person—body, mind and spirit—the journey and process of which has led this author to a more meaningful, fulfilled, and loving life. I trust it will do the same for you.

I dedicate this book to my sons, Brent and Mark, with the prayer that their lives will be greatly enriched as they, too, face and help break the chain from generations past.

Richard (Dick) Innes
San Clemente, California

*"Only to the degree that we are
made whole will our lifestyle,
our actions, our attitudes, and our
relationships be wholesome."*

1

A Time to Love
A Time to Heal

"I'M THE KIND OF MAN you love to hate!"

These were the words of a man I will call Fred spoken at a live-in weekend retreat-workshop. He stood alone in the center of a circle completely surrounded by some eighty men. He was visibly and understandably shaken, his breathing was difficult, his face was flushed, and he was perspiring profusely as he told us his agonizing story.

It took tremendous courage to do what Fred did, given the company he was in—most of whom were church members who, sad to say, are sometimes more inclined to give people the "left foot of fellowship" (rather than the right hand) if they confess their faults and sins, especially if the sins are of a sexual nature. There was deathly silence as Fred shared what to him was a lifelong struggle. Not as much as a murmur could be heard. All eyes were riveted on a man whose greatest strength was to admit his weakness. With his face in his hands—terrified of rejection—Fred shared that he was a homosexual.

Once we knew his background we could understand why he became what he was. He grew up in a home where his father was a traveling salesman and rarely at home. His mother, to meet her needs, who according to Fred was a well-endowed woman, made him sleep with her every night for a number of years when he was growing up and regularly seduced him into fondling her.

Fred was overwhelmed by his mother's overpowering seduction. His father's failure to protect and "wean" him from her clutches, and to be there for him to identify with, added to his despair. In his desperate search for love, he turned to homosexual relationships in a vain attempt to get his father-need met and his mother-wound healed.

To complicate matters Fred sought help to overcome his problem and was seduced by his male "counselor." Despairing of life, he went to the top of a high building intending to jump off and end it all. Fortunately, a seemingly "invisible hand" reached out and stopped him.

Fred turned to God for help but also needed the help and support of loving people that he could trust. Because he had been hurt deeply by an absentee father, an incestuous mother, and an unsafe "counselor," it was extremely difficult for him to trust again and reach out to anyone for help.

Fortunately he did. And a vital part of his recovery was the day he again took the risk of being rejected when he made himself incredibly vulnerable and shared his story with us. I don't think there was a dry eye in that circle. Not one of us judged, condemned, or rejected Fred. We loved and accepted him because he was being open and real, and genuinely wanted to be healed.

Had we judged, condemned, preached at (which can be a not-too-subtle form of judgment and a show of self-right-eousness), or rejected Fred in any way, we would have added to his self-rejection and, in turn, reinforced his temptation to keep looking for love in all the wrong ways and places.

All behavior is caused

The truth is that negative behavior, relational conflicts, and many physical ills—the presenting problems that we see—are often the symptoms or the fruit of deeply buried and hidden roots. In other words, so many of our problems have a cause or causes behind them, causes that are often multiple, complex, and hidden.

While most of us may not have been wounded emotionally to the degree that Fred had been, many have been; some have been hurt even more, and almost all of us have been hurt or damaged to some degree.

Our society is filled with people with broken wings—young and old alike—caused not only by sexual and/or physical abuse, but also by emotional abuse, spiritual abuse, rejection, abandonment, or neglect in one form or another—all of which boil down in some way to a failure in love. The effects can be devastating and are revealed in feelings of inferiority, insecurity, anxiety, loneliness, unhappiness, depression, impaired relationships, divorce, multiple marriages, wounded spirits, addictive behaviors, illicit sex, pornography, abortion, anger, and all sorts of other self-destructive behaviors—plus physical ills that are caused or greatly aggravated by supercharged repressed negative and damaged emotions.

The reality is that most, if not all, of us are wounded to some degree—some more, some less. True, while many have wonderful childhood memories, none of us had a perfect upbringing or received perfect love because none of us had perfect parents. Furthermore, we are all born with a sinful nature with a bias towards sinning. Many, too, have been sinned against in some way. As one of my mentors, the late Dr. Cecil Osborne, used to say, "Everybody either has a problem, lives with a problem, or is a problem!"

As long as we have any unresolved personal problems,

11

character issues, negative or sinful habits, addictions, broken relationships, false or real guilt, hidden fears, spiritual emptiness, personal conflicts, or physical ills that are caused or greatly aggravated by unresolved emotional pain, or as long as we are not fulfilled in love, we are like a bird trying to fly with a broken wing—and have a need for healing.

That's that bad news. The good news is that God doesn't want us to stay this way. His goal is that we are healed and made whole. As Jesus said to sick and hurting people, "Do you want to be made well/whole?"[1] What we need to realize is that only to the degree that we are made whole will our life, actions, attitudes, relationships, and our love be wholesome. God wants us to rise up and soar on wings like eagles so that we will reach the heights of all that he planned and envisioned for us to become and do.

We have God's promise that "those who hope in the LORD will renew their strength. They will soar on wings like eagles; they will run and not grow weary, they will walk and not be faint."[2]

With God's help, our own committed effort, and the help and support of non-judgmental, safe people we can achieve this goal.

Footnotes:

1. John 5:6.
2. Isaiah 40:31 (NIV).

"Don't ask me to run.
I can't.
My leg is broken."

2

Broken Wings
Shattered Dreams

I HADN'T PLAYED TENNIS since my youth and decided to take it up again. I thought I could pick up where I left off more years ago than I wish to remember. Wrong. In my very first game I made a sudden lurch sideways to reach for a ball and crack, something in my right leg snapped and my leg gave way beneath me. Like the two frayed ends of a broken rope my Achilles tendon had snapped in two.

Even more frustrating was the fact that when I had been out of the cast only a few weeks, and was anxious to be active again, I was on my mountain bike. Instead of riding across a very busy intersection, I waited for the light to change to carefully walk across the street. As I stepped off the pavement on the "walk light" a car swung around the corner on my left and, startled, I jumped out of the way—and snapped the same tendon again!

While my leg was in a cast and I was getting around on crutches, nobody expected me to run, play any kind of active sports, or do any heavy physical work. People didn't place any such expectations on me because it was obvious I couldn't do these things with a broken leg. I never had to say, "Don't ask me to run. I can't. My leg is broken."

However, when it comes to everyday living and we appear whole and healthy there are often unrealistic expectations placed on us. This is especially true if we belong to certain religious groups or a particular culture. The degree of the expectations will vary depending on the group to which we belong. Far too often we are expected to "fly with a broken wing" because our brokenness can't be seen. That is, we are expected to live victoriously regardless of our damaged emotions and wounded heart, and to conform to others' expectations of us.

Whether we are Amish, Baptist, Catholic, Charismatic, Church of Christ, Episcopalian, Jehovah's Witness, Jewish, Methodist, Mormon, Muslim, Presbyterian, Uniting Church, or whatever, makes no difference in that every group has its spoken or unspoken, subtle or not-so-subtle, expectations. Even in liberal groups you are expected to be liberal—they too can be very rigid in their expectations! And the more rigid the group, the more rigid are the expectations. If we conform and live up to these expectations—realistic or not—we'll be accepted. And, if we don't, we won't!

To be or not to be accepted

Rigid "do's" and "don'ts" are symptoms of legalism which, in any form, are destructive as they are a defense against facing one's reality. Paul said to the Christians in Galatia when they slipped back into a legalistic form of religion, "Who has bewitched or bedeviled you?"[1] Unfortunately, people who are theologically rigid interpret their rigidity as spirituality. They believe adhering to legalistic rules makes them spiritual. They don't realize that they are theologically rigid because

16

they are emotionally rigid and immature, and that they are exercising a certain degree of self-righteousness.

While I'm extremely grateful for the many benefits gained from my Christian upbringing, I've had to sort out the real from the false in order to find freedom in my faith and personal life, as I came from a minimally legalistic, religious background. There were a few unrealistic expectations placed on us by our church that were reinforced by our families. To be accepted we were expected to adhere to certain "do's" and "don'ts."

When we became a little older, we used to joke not-so-kindly that we couldn't do this and we couldn't do that—we couldn't go here and we couldn't go there—neither could the people in the cemetery because they were dead too. Some of these expectations were not necessarily wrong in and of themselves, but they were used to grade the depth of our spirituality and describe what a good Christian was or was not.

While expectations have changed with the changing times, there are still unrealistic expectations—subtle or otherwise—placed on many Christians and religious people today. When it's all boiled down, however, all of these are a means of avoiding one's reality (seeing ourselves as God sees us), and are often used as a means of controlling people. They can be stifling, if not crippling, to both spiritual and emotional well-being.

Do's and don'ts

❑ *Faithful church attendance*

In my youthful days very important among the "do's" was faithful attendance at most, if not all, of our weekly church services, which was supposedly another indication of one's spirituality—especially if we attended the midweek prayer meeting. Here we always prayed on our knees (fortunately with a cushion). As a teen this made it easy for me to use the cushion as a pillow and lay "prostrate" on the floor beneath a pew, where I couldn't be seen by the honorable reverend, and catch up on lost sleep! In other words, spirituality was measured more by outward appearances rather than the attitude of one's heart.

❏ *Getting "the blessing"*

On one occasion I got caught napping with my head down, not in a prayer meeting hiding beneath a pew, but in the middle of a Sunday worship service in view of the entire congregation! The night before I had been fishing all night (no lie) and hadn't had any sleep before attending church. In every worship service we always had what was called a "season of prayer" and on this particular Sunday, during the season of prayer, I laid my head on my folded arms on the back of the pew in front of me appearing to be in a prayerful posture—and promptly fell sound asleep. When the "season of prayer" ended, I didn't. I don't know how long I appeared to be praying, but I was awakened by a group of men, all of whom had hands laid on me praying fervently for me. I think they thought I was getting "the blessing" as I belonged to a church where such was vital for being fully accepted, or at least to gain a feeling of belonging.

To say the least, I was profoundly shocked and no less embarrassed when I was awakened from my slumber. I confess that I never did confess to those men—or to anybody else in the church. The point is that until we got "the blessing" we were considered "less than" in our Christian faith and experience. The pressure to get "the blessing" was very intense which paved the way for many a "blessing" to be a counterfeit experience.

❏ *Witnessing*

Another expectation high on the list was that we were to "witness" regularly by verbally sharing our Christian faith which, by the way, I was scared to death to do and hated doing in the way I was taught, and have since written a book to make my point, a book with the tongue-in-cheek title, *I Hate Witnessing*! I discovered I had no shortage of friends in this arena.

If we didn't "witness" regularly (which most of us didn't do, including those who told us we should), we were made to feel guilty. In fact, much of our life was controlled by false guilt—the "gift that keeps on giving!"

Unfortunately, I ended up taking in these unrealistic expectations and placing them on myself. The smallest slip-up would send me on a guilt trip. As somebody said (also with tongue-in-cheek): "My mother was my travel agent who sent me on my guilt trips." For me it was more my church and to some degree my father rather than my mother. In fact, even as an adult for a long time I thought that if I committed certain sins, God would kill me! Not a noble motive to live a "holy" life I might add! However, as I eventually learned, it wasn't God who I feared would kill me, but my father. I had projected my childish fear of him onto God, the Heavenly Father, a practice that many are prone to do.

❏ No Problems

Another unrealistic expectation, which is still true for many Christians today, was that if we were truly spiritual, we shouldn't have any major problems, or if we did and trusted God, he would take care of them. The panacea or cure-all for such was to trust God, be "in the Word" (that is, be regularly reading and studying the Bible), have a daily devotional prayer time, and be filled with the Holy Spirit.

Even one of my college professors taught that a Christian should never get depressed. I won't take time to discuss Elijah and his experience following his incredible victory at

Mt. Carmel over the three hundred prophets of Baal, after which he despaired of life and wanted to die, except to ask: Did God say to Elijah in his hour of despair, "Rise, pray, and read your Bible?" No, of course not. God simply said, "Rise and eat!"

Elijah was depressed because he was exhausted physically, emotionally, and spiritually. Furthermore, he was afraid for his life as Queen Jezebel was determined to have him killed. Depression was a fairly normal response under such circumstances. What Elijah needed at this time was a good feed and a good rest—and to hide out for a while!

I have a good friend who suffers from depression. Before his problem was diagnosed as bipolar, which is a chemical deficiency in the brain, well-meaning but ill-informed Christians led him to believe his problem was demonic. This of course, stopped him getting his problem correctly diagnosed and increased his depression.

I'm sure that most people who give simplistic solutions and pat "Biblical" answers for resolving many of life's complex problems mean well. They can be very sincere but far from the truth and quite rigid in their thinking. For rigid people, their "only tool is a hammer and they tend to see every problem as a nail!" That is, they have the same simplistic solution for every problem. The trouble is not every problem is a "nail" and in fact, none are.

Trying to fly with a broken wing

Because of unrealistic expectations placed on people, many are unwittingly lured into denial and compelled to pretend outwardly what they aren't feeling on the inside. Consequently they are fearful to admit their secret sins, personal failures, and problems for fear of being judged and/or even rejected.

❏ *What you see may not be*

Speaking of myself, because I looked okay on the outside and could perform well in my work and because I appeared to have it "all together" it was assumed, first by others and then by myself, that I could live up to the expectations that were placed on me. And from my youth up I genuinely tried to do so.

But I didn't have it all together. Just as when my leg was broken and I couldn't run, neither could I live up to unrealistic expectations because I was broken on the inside! The difference between my broken leg and my broken "inner self" was that one you could see, the other you couldn't!

I couldn't live a wholesome life because I wasn't whole and I could only put on an outward act for so long. Eventually it caught up with me. Only when my world crumbled did I see that I was broken and needed "fixing" (healing)—from the inside out, not the outside in!

❏ *You can't give what you haven't got*

Furthermore, being broken on the inside I wasn't able to fully love—the ultimate need and desire of every person and certainly the goal for every genuine Christian. How could I love and accept anybody else in a healthy way when I didn't love and accept myself in a healthy way? I couldn't. To expect being able to do so was an unrealistic expectation I had placed on myself. It is impossible to give what we don't have.

Nobody can run with a broken leg any more than a bird can fly with a broken wing. Neither can anybody live a love-filled life when he or she is broken on the inside. To expect otherwise is not only unrealistic but is a fantasy that leads to a sense of failure and despair—or forces one into denial where he can easily hide behind a facade of religiosity or any of a number of other self-protective defenses.

God's goals versus man's

It's others (and often we ourselves) who put unrealistic expectations and impossible goals on us. Not God. When it comes to interpreting God's Word, we always see it from our vantage point and interpret it on the basis of our biases. As another has said, "We see things not the way they are but the way we are." In fact, the more out of touch we are with our own reality; that is, the more untruthful (dishonest) we are with our inner selves (our true feelings and motives), the more we will distort all other truth, including God's truth, and twist it to match our perception of reality.

The opposite is also true. The more in touch with and the more honest we are with our inner selves, the clearer we will see God's truth and all other truth and reality.

When we are unreal and rigid, like the Pharisees of Christ's day, we set up rules and expectations to avoid facing our inner brokenness and to keep ourselves feeling safe and protected. And then we claim that these rules and expectations are from God.

The following expectations, which are as real today as they were when I was growing up, are two more that are man-made. They may sound very spiritual and noble but are in reality the enemy of reality. They keep people in bondage, confuse their thinking and beliefs, and cause them to be defeated in daily living.

❑ *God's goal is to make us good ...really?*

The first of these two unrealistic expectations is that it is God's goal to make us good. However, as contradictory as it may sound, God's goal is not to make us good—for goodness sake. His goal is to make us whole, to heal and fix us on the inside—to mend our broken heart, our damaged emotions, and our broken lives. The goodness that God wants of us is to be the fruit of this. Wholesome living with the right motives can only come as a result of our being made whole.

While it is true that Jesus came to seek and to save the lost, he never invited or asked anyone if they wanted to be saved, but rather, "Do you want to be made well? Do you want to be made whole?"[2] Repeatedly, when Jesus healed people, the Gospel records say they were made whole. And that's God's goal for us. Actually, in the original text of the New Testament in several instances the word translated "saved" can be equally translated "well" or "whole."

At the beginning of his earthly ministry Jesus announced: "The Spirit of the Lord is upon me; he has appointed me to preach Good News to the poor; he has sent me to heal the brokenhearted and to announce that captives shall be released...."[3]

It wasn't to make us good but to heal us and make us whole.

❏ God's goal is to make us moral ... oh?

Second, closely related to the false expectation that God's goal to make us good is that it is also God's goal to make us moral. As another has said, "God isn't into morality. He's into reality," meaning that his goal is not to make us moral but to make us real before we become moral.

None of us can be totally good or totally moral in our own strength or through our own efforts. A misunderstanding of this principle is perhaps one of the reasons we see moral lapses among Christians.

The moralists of Christ's day were the religious Pharisees. Their goodness, morality, and their piousness were an outward show used as a smoke screen to avoid seeing their inner brokenness and admitting what they were on the inside. Jesus didn't have kind words to say to them. In fact he lambasted their phony religiosity. "Woe upon you, Pharisees, and you other religious leaders—hypocrites! For you tithe down to the last mint leaf in your garden, but ignore the important things—justice and mercy and faith. Yes, you should tithe, but you shouldn't leave the more important things undone. Blind guides! You strain out a gnat and swallow a camel. Woe to you, Pharisees, and you religious leaders—hypocrites! You are so careful to polish the outside of the cup, but the inside is foul with extortion and greed. Blind Pharisees! First cleanse the inside of the cup, and then the whole cup will be clean. Woe to you, Pharisees, and you religious leaders! You are like beautiful mausoleums—full of dead men's bones, and of foulness and corruption. You try to look like saintly men, but underneath those pious robes of yours are hearts besmirched with every sort of hypocrisy and sin."[4]

Whew—quite a mouthful from the Son of God. But what Jesus was saying is that God hates religious phoniness. He wants us to be real and see and admit to our brokenness so he can fix and heal us on the inside. When this is taken care of, our external actions will be a reflection of what we are on the inside.

To act perfectly outwardly without cleaning up the inside first is what God hates because the actions are just a show and no healing, growth, or recovery can happen. Instead of being enlightened and seeing the truth, we remain "en-darkened" locked in a prison of self-deception.

God wants us to be made whole in body, mind, and spirit—and as medical science has discovered, these parts of our person are interrelated. In other words, the healthier I become spiritually and emotionally, the healthier I will be physically, the healthier and more loving I will be in my relationships, and the healthier my outward actions will be.

No pat answers

Unfortunately, what many Christians today either haven't been shown or don't fully grasp is that we don't overcome "bad" by being "good" or achieve spirituality by living an outwardly moral life. To overcome sinful habits and personal problems we need to feel loved and affirmed by God the Heavenly Father at the very core of our being, and with his help, to be made whole. Simplistic solutions and "quick-fix-Band-Aid" answers to resolve life's complex problems simply do not work, and often drive sincere strugglers into deeper despair.

❏ Nice sounding words—misleading advice

For example, not so long ago I read the following advice in a daily devotional published by a highly respected and well-known Christian organization. The article read, "When we become aware that we're plunging into sin, we must immediately stop the slide by ceasing to do evil. But that's not enough. We need to call on Christ our Rescuer, confess our sin and forsake it, receive by faith God's mercy and pardon, and go on with the Lord. Then, as we place ourselves under the authority of God's Word, we will be back on the path of righteousness with a mind at peace and a heart filled with joy."[5] Wouldn't it be nice if it were that simple?

Another issue of the same devotional said, "We tend to forget that Jesus also died to make us good."[6] Still another issue declared, "When a person has so much [success] and is still bitterly dissatisfied—even suicidal—what's not there? A relationship with God."[7] And still another article claimed, "All around us are people who could have ... peace and contentment if they could just meet Jesus."[8]

I also recall a famous preacher claiming that all one had to do to overcome loneliness was to give his or her life to Jesus.

Again, I wish the answer to overcoming sin, addictions, self-destructive behaviors, impaired relationships, and loneliness and finding inner peace, joy, and contentment were that simple. It isn't. It may sound spiritual but it's not reality—and what is not reality is not spiritual. Like many teachings, while they may contain an element of truth (which makes them believable), they sound great as long as you don't need them!

❏ *If only...*

If these simple solutions were true, there would be fewer empty, unhappy, unfulfilled, defeated, hurting, lonely and depressed Christians—as I was to some degree for many years even though I was doing all the "right" things outwardly, including trusting Jesus, having a daily devotional time, and serving God in full-time Christian service no less! Trusting Jesus gave me peace with God, but not with myself. That had to come through the healing of my damaged emotions and broken inner self.

Furthermore, if these simplistic answers worked, there would be many more happy marriages and considerably fewer divorces among Christians.

To tell me when I am "plunging" into sin that I must immediately stop the slide by ceasing to do evil is like telling me to pick myself up by my bootstraps. Also, if I could stop the slide by myself, I wouldn't need Jesus or God's help. And to tell me that I will find joy and peace and overcome my loneliness by trusting Jesus, without my facing and treating the root cause or causes of my plight, is about as helpful as telling a sick person to stop being sick without treating the cause of his sickness—or expecting someone to run with a broken leg, or a bird to fly with a broken wing! Such is impossible.

How sad it is when these lofty, unrealistic ideals and impossible expectations are handed down from the pulpit.

❏ *The fail trail*

This kind of teaching is fine if you're not sick or don't need it. But for those among us who know we are strugglers it can leave us frustrated, disillusioned, defeated, depressed and/or guilt-ridden (false guilt-ridden that is). It can add to our sense of failure and feelings of inadequacy and causes some to abandon their faith.

Jesus never told us to overcome negative behavior and sinful or self-destructive behaviors by "ceasing to do evil" or by "placing ourselves under the authority of God's Word" as "spiritual" as these may sound (and as important as these are in the right context). Overcoming our brokenness is not that easy. We act out in unhealthy ways because we are unhealthy and need to be healed. We act out in sinful ways because we are broken sinners and need fixing. And we act out in self-destructive ways and hurt other people because we've been hurt and lack a healthy sense of self-love. To love in healthy ways, we need to have our damaged emotions healed and our "broken parts" fixed.

❏ *The success way*

Jesus made the way to overcoming sin and human problems implicitly clear—though difficult to follow. When a lawyer, attempting to trap Jesus in matters of the law, asked him what the greatest commandment was, Jesus replied, "'Love the Lord your God with all your heart, soul, and mind.' This is the first and greatest commandment. The second most important is similar: 'Love your neighbor as much as you love yourself.' All the other commandments ... stem from these two laws and are fulfilled if you obey them. Keep only these and you will find that you are obeying all the others."[9]

In other words, when we truly love God, our neighbor, and ourselves—as God loves us—only then can we live healthy and good lives and fulfill all of God's laws and commandments. To love in this way we need to be healed within and made whole, which is not a simple or single event but rather a process of growth and maturity. It also involves facing the

27

causes of our problems and working through and resolving these issues, which takes time and a lot of hard work. True, our salvation is a gift from God but with his help it is our responsibility to work out that salvation in our daily lives.[10]

Nobody expects a broken radio to work. It may look perfect on the outside but when the inside is broken, it can't work. Neither can we. To expect otherwise is to set ourselves up for failure, discouragement, and shattered dreams.

❏ *Facing reality*

The fact is we are all sick to some degree. We are all broken. We are all sinners. We all have wounded hearts and some damaged emotions. That's why God sent his Son to save us and set us free! It should go without saying that only those who admit their sickness and brokenness can ever be healed and made whole. As Jesus said to the Pharisees, "It is not the healthy who need a doctor, but the sick. I have not come to call the righteous, but sinners to repentance."[11]

Only to the degree that I admit my sickness, brokenness, and need for healing can I ever be healed and made whole. And then, only to the degree that I am made whole will my lifestyle, my actions, my attitudes, and my relationships be whole-some (wholesome). And only to the degree that I feel loved will I be loving.

❏ *A process—not an event*

Healing the wounded person is a process, not an event. It's a journey of the heart, mind and soul. We took x number of years to become who we are and we don't change that overnight. Being made whole is a result of growing up into the fullness of our salvation and going on to maturity in every area of life. The biblical term is sanctification—and there is no such thing as instant sanctification or instant maturity. To expect such is another unrealistic expectation and can be a handy excuse to hang onto if we don't want to face reality and grow up.

Growth, wholeness, maturity, sanctification, recovery (by whatever name you call it) is not an event—it's a process, a journey. It's simple, but it isn't easy. That is, the principles are simple but applying them to our daily lives can be very challenging and painful at times, but also very rewarding. Only those who are willing to face their reality and pay the price will ever find the healing and wholeness that God has envisioned for them. Like climbing a mountain, when we experience the magnificent view from the top, we realize that the climb has been worth every ounce of effort we put into it. Likewise, the rewards for growing on toward maturity and finding wholeness are also worth every effort put into the journey and the process. Only then can the desires of our heart and our deepest dreams become a reality.

Footnotes:

1. Galatians 3:1.
2. John 5:6.
3. Luke 4:18, (TLB).
4. Matthew 23:23-28, (TLB).
5. *Our Daily Bread*, (Grand Rapids, MI 49555: Radio Bible Class,1993), Vol. 38, July 28, 1993.
6. Ibid, July 21, 1994.
7. Ibid, July 09, 1994.
8. Ibid, December 23, 1994.
9. Matthew 23:37-40, (thb).
10. Philippians 2:12-13.
11. Luke 5:31-32, (NIV).

Change is tough. If you're like most people, every fibre of your being will resist having to take on the hard work of eliminating the thoughts that support your self-forfeiting feelings and behavior.

3

Your Healing
Is Within You

IT IS SAID THAT Alfred Adler, the famous psychoanalyst, would ask each client at the close of his initial consultation, "And what would you do if you were cured?" After the patient would give his answer, Adler would get up, open the door and reply, "Well, go do it then."

While there is a time for analysis, there is also a time for action. Keep in mind that when it comes to healing we need to think in terms of healing the whole person—emotional and spiritual as well as the physical—and realize there is much we can and need to do ourselves, things that God isn't going to do for us, because if he did, he would be keeping us over-dependent and immature.

Also, is it God's will for everybody to be healed physically, emotionally and spiritually? Some people think so. Others think not. Some aren't sure.

Regarding physical healing, the Apostle Paul, the most influential leader of the early Christian church, had a problem that he didn't name. He referred to it as his "thorn in the flesh." Some scholars think this "thorn" may have been a physical problem or weakness. Whatever it was, it was something that bothered him, but God didn't heal him or deliver him from it. Paul had some very unusual spiritual experiences that made a profound impact on his life. Because of these he said God allowed this "thorn" to keep him humble. "Three times," Paul said, "I pleaded with the Lord to take it away from me. But he said to me, 'My grace is sufficient for you, for my power is made perfect in weakness.'"[1]

In Christ's day many people were healed but, like Paul, not all were. Dorcas, one of the women active in the early church was raised from the dead.[2] But John the Baptist, the man who paved and prepared the way for Christ's ministry, lost his head and stayed dead. Tradition has it that all Jesus' disciples met with an untimely and cruel death except for John who was banished to the Isle of Patmos in his latter days.

Regarding emotional healing, Luke, the physician disciple, told how Jesus healed the woman who had suffered for eighteen years from a "spirit of infirmity"[3] which some believe was an emotional problem—not a demon. This is because Jesus never laid hands on anyone who was possessed with a demon. He did lay his hands on this woman and healed her of both her emotional and physical problem. This is an important observation because many of our physical ills are either caused or greatly aggravated by unresolved emotional problems.

The problem of suffering

❏ *Benefits*

Keep in mind, too, that it's through suffering that many, if not most, of life's great achievements have come. It's also in the valleys and not on the mountaintops where we learn the most. It's the tough times that make people tough. It's not that God causes suffering but he certainly allows people, including his most faithful followers, to experience and go through it. Suffering, if we allow it to, teaches us to understand life and equips us to be more effective people helpers.

Many of the Psalms were written out of David's times of despair, failures, and fears. He was understandably afraid for his life when King Saul who, out of intense jealousy and envy, was hunting him down to kill him. The Apostle Paul wrote several of his New Testament letters when in prison. Jesus' closest friend and disciple, John, wrote the book of Revelation when he was isolated on the Isle of Patmos.

John Bunyan wrote his famous book, *Pilgrim's Progress*, when he was in prison. And when poet Elizabeth Barrett married fellow poet Robert Browning, her parents so strongly disapproved that they disowned her. In a vain attempt to reconcile to them, Elizabeth wrote to them weekly for years. Ten years later she received a package in the mail and upon opening it found every letter she had written to her parents returned—unopened. Those letters are among the most beautiful in English literature. It's sad to think of it, but had her parents read some of those letters and had they been reconciled, many of those letters would never have been written and many, perhaps all, would never have been read by anyone else.

❏ *Suffering that's difficult to understand*

If it were God's will to heal all sickness, one would think his choicest servants would be among the first to be healed. But it isn't so. One of the church's great contemporary spokesmen, perhaps one of the most influential of all time, is Dr. Billy Graham. He has preached the gospel to more people than anyone else. If God would protect anyone from sickness or heal them from it, one would expect that Billy Graham would be one of them. It's sad to think that he is afflicted with Parkinson's disease. Imagine the thousands of prayers that have been offered on his behalf but he hasn't been healed. I saw him at his crusade in San Diego and it was sad to see this great man of God barely able to walk without assistance. But God's anointing was still very evident. The number of people who responded to the invitation to accept Christ as their Savior was staggering. And some years ago Dr. Graham's song-leader, Cliff Barrows, lost his first wife, Billie, through cancer.

A much younger and very talented friend of mine who is active and faithful in Christian ministry recently learned that she has MS. Many prayers have been offered on her behalf too, but she hasn't been healed and her condition is worsening.

While writing this chapter I received a telephone call to let me know that a mutual friend's two-and-a-half-year-old son who had been ill for many months, passed away that morning. The mother grew up on the mission field and ever since, with her husband, has been active in Christian service. Many prayers didn't heal or save her child.

❏ *Suffering is part of the human condition*

As already stated, we live in a broken world and as the Scriptures say, the sun rises on both good and evil people, and rain falls on the just equally as it does on the unjust.[4] As one humorist put it, "It rains on the just and on the unjust fella, but more on the just because the unjust has the just's umbrella!" And there is often truth in that. It's a fact of life that good things happen to bad people and bad things happen to good people—and vice versa.

We suffer because we are human. We get sick because that is a part of the human condition. Some people go through life with few ills, others with many. Some get well. Others don't. Even leaders in the healing ministry get sick and don't get healed. One of these men in Australia died of a heart attack while still relaively young. Another in England died of cancer. Another prominent leader in the healing ministry in North America also died of cancer. Nobody is immune.

In spite of this, I still believe it is God's will for most, if not all of us, to be healthier than many of us are; that is, healthier in body, mind, and spirit and thereby add years to our life. But this will only happen if we genuinely want to be made whole and are prepared to do what we need to do to make it happen. When we apply the following principles for healing and wholeness, a more contented and healthier life is all but guaranteed.

The will to get well

"Do you want to get well?" What a seemingly dumb question to ask a helpless man who had been handicapped for thirty-eight years. But that's exactly what Jesus asked a man he found with many other ill people at the Pool of Bethesda in old Jerusalem town.

I have no idea why Jesus asked only one of the many sick people on that occasion if he wanted to get well. Regardless, this man replied to Jesus' question, "Sir, I have no one to help me into the pool when the water is stirred. While I am trying to get in, someone else goes down ahead of me."

"Then Jesus said to him, 'Get up! Pick up your mat and walk.' At once the man was cured; he picked up his mat and walked."[5] Obviously this man wanted to be healed. Maybe he was the only one there at the pool who did and that's why Jesus asked him if he wanted to be healed?

❏ *Few there be that find it*

One would imagine that the majority of sick patients would want to get well, but according to Dr. Bernie S. Siegel, author of the book *Love, Medicine and Miracles*, this isn't so.

According to Siegel's study about fifteen to twenty percent of sick people don't want to get better. For some, sickness is a way to get sympathy and attention. Not feeling loved and not knowing how to get it, they mistake attention for love. To get well would spoil their self-deceptive ploy. Some even wish to die. This way they wouldn't have to face life with its many responsibilities anymore.

A further sixty to seventy percent of patients depend almost entirely on their doctor to make them better. They become passive conformists to the doctor's directions. If given a choice, they would rather be operated on than "operate" on themselves.[6] When Siegel offers these people "a choice between an operation and a change in lifestyle, eight out of ten say, 'Operate. It hurts less. That way all I have to do is get a babysitter for the week I'm in the hospital.'"[7]

Only fifteen to twenty percent of all patients are willing to take an active part in their own healing. These are the patients Siegel calls exceptional and are the ones who are committed to and get involved in their own healing. They want to understand everything about their condition and the treatment they are given, and are not always appreciated by their physicians. They ask a lot of questions and express their emotions freely. But these patients have the highest rate of recovery. They want to get well.[8]

❏ *What more do you expect?*

When it comes to healing emotional ills, the former Minirth-Meier counseling group, one of the largest Christian counseling organizations in the nation, and whose clients were mostly Christian, found similar results. Their "therapist's best guesstimate was that only twenty-five percent of all Minirth-Meier clients want to find out the truth [the cause of their problems], and even fewer want to deal with it. Most patients visit the clinic looking for quick and easy solutions. They want a pill to make their anxiety go away. Or they want a counselor to listen to their problems and then blame them on someone else. The last thing a patient wants to hear is that his own anger or guilt or jealousy is the source of his anxiety and that he is responsible for getting rid of the negative emotions [that are causing his or her illness or conflicts]."[9]

These people, even though they verbally admit to having a problem and appear to want help, rationalize at least to themselves, "I'm going to a counselor. What more do you expect?"

❏ *A fighting spirit*

Wanting to get well of itself is not enough to make healing happen, but it is the next step for healing after one admits that he or she has a problem. The Australians have a wonderful word for people who really mean business—it's fair-dinkum. Those who are fair-dinkum about their healing not only want to get well, but also have a "fighting spirit" and don't give up. As Seigel shared, "A group of London researchers under Keith Pettingale reported a ten-year survival rate of seventy-five percent among cancer patients who reacted to the diagnosis with a 'fighting spirit,' compared with a twenty-two percent survival rate among those who responded with 'stoic acceptance' or feelings of helplessness or hopelessness."[10]

According to Doctors Seigel, Minirth and Meier less than one-quarter of medical patients and counseling clients have this "fighting spirit" in that they are prepared to do what they need to do in order to get well; that is, accept responsibility for their recovery. These findings parallel Jesus' parable about the four soils—the wayside soil, the stony soil, the thorny soil, and the good soil. Each soil represents a type of person. Only the good soil produced lasting results. Some of the others started out well, but soon fizzled out.[11]

Just as many want the doctor or counselor to give them a quick fix, many want God to give them a quick fix, too. When he doesn't, they become disillusioned. It would be nice if healing were that simple and worked that way. But it rarely does.

Determination

According to counselor and author, Dave Carder, many people in a twelve-step recovery movement also want a quick fix. When they don't find it, they also became dis-illusioned. I'm a great believer in the twelve-step program based on the AA approach. It has helped and is helping millions of people. But it isn't enough just to talk about problems and hope they will go away. One not only needs to admit his addiction or problem and bring it to the light, but also needs to look at and resolve the root cause/s beneath the presenting problem so he can deal with it at its source.

Fixing a root canal in a tooth can be extremely painful. Fixing "root canals" in emotional and other aches can be equally painful. Only those who truly want to recover and get well—and are determined to do so—will.

The greatest healer of all time, Jesus Christ, knew that if people were going to find healing, they had to want it. As already noted, his question to those who came to him for help was simple, straightforward, and direct. "Do you want to get well? Do you want to be made whole?" he asked.[12] If people don't want or are not determined to get well, to grow, and to change, there is little, if anything, anyone can do for them—including God. He has given us freedom of choice and never imposes his will or help on anyone. Only those who admit they have a problem and genuinely want help and are determined, with God's help, to do what they need to do in order to get well, can be helped and healed.

❏ *Wants versus wishes*

As indicated, desire plus determination are essential for finding healing and wholeness, but sometimes we only think we want these. Take, for example, people who say they want to lose weight. Every time I ask this question in a workshop or seminar, many hands are raised. But how many are actually telling the truth?

Unless we have a metabolism or other biological problem, we pretty much weigh about what we want to. None of us eat anything we don't want to eat. The question is: What do we want most—to eat right and exercise regularly or just eat? We may say we want to weigh less, but unless we accept responsibility to do what we need to do to weigh less (including resolving any causes behind bad eating habits), our want is only a wish. And there's all the difference in the world between a want and a wish. To turn a wish into a want takes not only strong desire and determination, but also action! It's what we do, not what we say, that counts.

I live at the top of a long and very steep hill—it's a mile to the bottom. To help keep my weight in check I regularly ride my mountain bike on our hill as I call it. Joy, my wife, likes to say to me when I go riding, "Have fun." The only fun is going down the hill. Riding up it is a long, arduous haul. But I love having ridden it. That's because of the results and the effect it has on me. Emotional healing is the same. It can be a long, arduous haul—but the results are incredibly rewarding—and well worth the struggle.

❏ *Change is tough*

Dr. Wayne Dyer, author of *Your Erroneous Zones* points out

how few people are willing to genuinely commit themselves to do what they need to do to bring about change in their life. He writes, "Looking at yourself in depth with an eye toward changing might be something that you say you are interested in accomplishing, but your behavior often speaks otherwise. Change is tough. If you're like most people, every fiber of your being will resist having to take on the hard work of eliminating the thoughts that support your self-forfeiting feelings and behavior."[13]

People who want to get well, "manifest the will to live in its most potent form. They take charge of their lives even if they were never able to before, and they work hard to achieve health and peace of mind. They do not rely on doctors to take the initiative but rather use them as members of a team, demanding the utmost in technique, resourcefulness, concern, and open-mindedness. If they're not satisfied, they change doctors."[14]

All the prayer in the world won't take away my excess weight, or resolve any other problem or sickness, that I am responsible for doing something about. To expect otherwise is a mark of immaturity. Worst of all is to blame my problem on the devil or a demon when the cure is in my hands. To do this is a handy excuse to hang on to if I don't want to get well and/or grow up.

If I genuinely want him to, God will help me see the cause or causes of my problems and lead me to the help I need, but he won't relieve me of personal responsibility. He will do for me what I cannot do for myself, but he won't do for me what I can and need to do for myself; otherwise, as already noted, he would be keeping me over-dependent and immature. I'm not talking about the willpower to overcome my problems in my own strength, but about accepting full responsibility to do what I need to do to get well.

❏ *Willing to be made willing*

Actually, whenever I have a problem that I can't resolve, regardless of what it is, I have learned the hard way to ask God to confront me with the truth and reality of what I may be contributing in any way to the situation I am in or the problem I am experiencing. Facing this reality can, at times, be very painful. Because of this, deep down I may not want to see what part I am playing. So when I pray such prayers, I tell God that I am willing to be made willing—no matter how much it hurts—for him to reveal to me whatever I need to see and ask him to give me the courage to do so. Only as I face and accept the truth about myself can I ever be set free. As Jesus so aptly put it, "You will know the truth, and the truth will set you free."[15]

By way of interest, I have "*never not*" had this prayer left unanswered. I know this is poor grammar, but it's a very effective and powerful way to pray. There have been times when I have had this prayer answered within an hour. On other issues it has taken several years—when I was ready and able to handle it. I wish I had learned to pray this prayer many years sooner. Could have saved myself many a headache and resolved a problem even years sooner. When we focus our prayers on the symptoms, we tend to reinforce them. When we focus them on the causes behind the symptoms, and want the truth, we are being honest with ourselves and honest with God. These are the prayers he delights to hear and answer, but he only answers them when we are ready, willing, and able to handle the truth—and genuinely want to see and know it. As the Bible says, "The Lord is near to all who call on him, to all who call on him in truth."[16]

Commitment

We have much to thank God for in the area of modern medical science, but there is much we can and need to do ourselves to overcome many of our physical and emotional ills, to maintain good health, and to discover physical, mental, and spiritual well-being.

Whatever the cause or causes of our illnesses, relational conflicts, or other personal problems, to get well and overcome these we need not only to strongly desire and be determined to get well, but also be absolutely committed to the process.

We may not have been responsible or to blame for what happened to us in the past that may have caused our problems, but we are totally responsible for what we do about resolving them. True, we may have been a victim in the past that caused some or many of our ills, but if we remain a victim, as another has said, we are now willing volunteers.

Desire, determination, and commitment are essential for overcoming any victim mentality, for rising above our circumstances, for discovering healing, wholeness, contentment, and genuine love, and to become the persons God envisioned us to be. When we do our part, God always does his. Thus, much of our healing is in our hands. The half-hearted never make it.

Footnotes:

1. 2 Corinthians 12:8-9, (NIV).
2. Acts 9:36-41.
3. Luke 13:11.
4. John 5:1-9, (NIV).
5. Matthew 5:45, (Paraphrase).
6. Bernie S. Siegel, M.D., *Love, Medicine and Miracles* (New York Harper and Row Publishers, Inc., 1986), 23-24.
7. Ibid, 3.
8. Ibid, 24.
9. Frank B. Minirth, M.D., Paul D. Meier, M.D., and Don Hawkins,Th.M., *Worry-free Living* (Nashville: Thomas Nelson Publishers,1989), 27-28.

10. Bernie S. Siegel, 25.

11. Matthew 13:3-8; 18-23.

12. John 5:6.

13. Dr. Duane W. Dyer, *Your Erroneous Zones* (London: Sphere Books Limited, 1976), 11.

14. Bernie S. Seigel, 3.

15. John 8:32, (NIV).

16. Psalm 145:18, (NIV).

"My role as a surgeon is to help [patients] get well and at the same time to understand why they became sick. Then they can go on to true healing, not merely a reversal of one particular disease."

4

Choice Not Chance Determines Destiny

TIM WAS A VERY CAPABLE man who had a very rewarding and profitable professional practice. His home was one of the largest and most opulent I had ever been in. He seemed to have just about everything a man could want to fulfill the American dream; that is, everything except happiness. His marriage was falling apart and his practice was beginning to slip as a result of his emotional condition. He was at wit's end when he came to me for counseling. For several weeks he spent the entire session berating his wife and telling me how terribly she was treating him.

I mostly listened. About all I had to say at the end of each session was, "That's not your problem."

"What do you mean, that's not my problem?" he demanded angrily.

"Come back next week and we'll talk more about it," I said.

We went through the same process for several weeks. He, berating his wife, and I, ending the session by telling him that his wife wasn't his problem. His relationship with her was merely the presenting problem—the one that motivated him to seek counseling which was a good thing.

Only when Tim was ready to face reality did the penny drop. When he stopped blaming his wife for his problems and looked within himself, he was able to see what the root cause of his problem was. He was extremely angry at his very critical and controlling mother. He had all sorts of negative feelings towards her from early childhood that he had never faced nor resolved, and was projecting these emotions onto his wife and taking them out on her. He came close to destroying his marriage. However, once he was willing to see the cause of his problem, he was able to confront and resolve it.

Resolution took some time and hard work, but the good news is that his marriage was saved. What is more, his wife decided to become a professional counselor so she could help other people resolve their conflicts.

The problem is "never" the problem

Like with Tim, more often than not, the problem we see is not the problem that is—and the pain we feel is not the pain that is. By this I mean that we tend to see only the symptom or presenting problem and feel the pain that this causes. When we see that our problem is the symptom of a deeper (often hidden) problem—the fruit of a deeper root—we can deal with the real problem which, in one form or another, is a failure in love.

Dr. Bernie Seigel agrees. He says, "The fundamental problem most patients face is an inability to love themselves, having been unloved by others during some crucial part of their lives. This period is almost always childhood, when our relations with our parents establish our characteristic ways of reacting to stress. As adults we repeat these reactions and make ourselves vulnerable to illness, and our personalities often determine the specific nature of the illnesses....

"My role as a surgeon," says Seigel, "is to ... help [patients] get well and at the same time to understand why they became sick. Then they can go on to true healing, not merely a reversal of one particular disease."[1]

True, some problems and ills we may need to live with, but many we don't. Either way, our destiny is decided by choice not chance. Choosing a healthy and positive attitude can greatly assist us to live with the problems we can't resolve and help us to change the ones we can change. That choice is ours. We can choose to stay sick or we can choose to get well and be made whole. Not to choose is a choice already made.

When I talk about a healthy positive attitude I'm not talking about denying reality. I'm talking about being a positive realist. If, for example, I've been hit by a truck, all the positive thinking in the world won't take away the pain. To be a positive realist I need to admit that I've been hit hard and am badly hurt, but will do everything I can, and get all the help I need, to recover. That's a conscious choice I need to make.

To recover, it is critical to identify the cause or causes of our ills and the problems we are experiencing so they can be dealt with and resolved. At the same time we need to get our basic needs for healthy living (healthy eating habits, rest and relaxation, and companionship) met in healthy ways, and eliminate as much as possible the things that add unnecessary stress that causes our physical, emotional, and relational ills to intensify.

Identifying causes

While it is important not to neglect treating symptoms, the critical issue is to identify and resolve the causes so we can get well. In fact, if we don't resolve the root cause/s of our problems, it is possible to be freed from one symptom and exchange it for another.

I recall hearing one speaker who claimed that God healed him from his alcoholism the moment he became a Christian. True, he may no longer be an alcoholic but to many of us it was obvious that he was now a "rage-aholic." All he had done was exchange one symptom for another.

The good news is that once we get beyond symptoms to find the cause or causes, we can pray intelligently, act responsibly, and get the proper help we need.

I don't deny that there are occasions when God does heal instantaneously, but most healing is a process. For instance, it takes six weeks for a broken bone to heal. It takes much longer for broken hearts, broken lives, and many other ills to heal. The time it takes depends much on the nature and cause of the illness or problem.

❏ *Physical symptoms*

In younger years I used to have bouts of hay fever every year and suffered from painful bursitis in both shoulders and couldn't raise my arms above my shoulders without feeling pain. I had no idea that these were both symptoms of deeper causes. Like many boys of my day I was taught that big men don't cry nor do they show hurt feelings. And somewhere along the line I learned, or perceived, that to be liked I needed to always be "nice" and not get angry. Wrong. Sure, I may have been liked—but I never felt loved. This was because the outer image I projected was not the real me.

It was the intense pain of a failed marriage that drove me into a recovery program. When I got connected to years of bottled-up grief and learned that it was okay to cry and sobbed buckets of tears, without knowing it I was being healed of my hay fever. Like, where do bottled up tears go?

We either express them as God intended, or we bury them and pay a high price for doing so. I can't help but wonder if one reason women live longer than men in Western society may be because it's acceptable for women to cry and express their feelings while we men feel that such is not acceptable nor manly. Just a thought.

Furthermore, I discovered that I also had a lot of repressed anger and when I got in touch with these feelings and learned to express them in healthy ways instead of internalizing them, I was healed of bursitis.

It is not without good reason that the Bible teaches the following principle: "Confess your sins [and faults] to each other and pray for each other so that you may be healed."[2]

One way to help identify the cause behind a problem is by tracing symptoms to their roots. Symptoms are a blessing in disguise. If I have a toothache or a pain in my arm, this is nature's way of telling me something is amiss and needs attention. Or as psychologist John Townsend puts it, "God is merciful. When we have unresolved problems, he gives us symptoms."

The reason symptoms can help reveal what the real problem is, is because they are often symbolic. For instance, one woman following a mastectomy said to her doctor, "I needed to get something off my chest!" Pity she didn't realize this long before it came to needing a mastectomy.

Pains in the shoulder can reflect the carrying of a heavy burden. Lower back pain can be symbolic of constantly bending over backwards to please everybody. Asthma, where a child finds it hard to breathe, may be the result of his or her feeling emotionally smothered by a smother-mother or father. Tension headaches can be from keeping anger in one's head. For me, hay fever proved to be from burying my grief.

If we have ulcers, what we eat can aggravate them, but not cause them. It's what's eating us that causes at least some ulcers. And if we have a pain in the neck, it may be because we are—or have someone in our life that is!

❏ *Behavioral symptoms*

Behavior, too, can be symbolic of a person's unresolved problems. A prostitute, for example, may be acting out her anger at and hatred of men. Many are incest victims who have been sexually abused by their father, uncle, or other significant male in their early life. In her anger she can be hitting back unconsciously at her father (or the one who victimized her) by becoming a prostitute.

In a similar way a man who is going from woman to woman and using them for his sexual gratification is just as likely to be acting out his anger towards his mother or other significant woman from his past who hurt, smothered, or neglected him—and because he is afraid to get close to a woman for fear of being hurt or smothered again. Only as these people resolve their past can they be fully released from their self-destructive ways of acting out.

❏ *Emotional symptoms*

The person who is saccharine sweet is usually very angry beneath his/her sickly sugary-sweet front. He who wants an inordinate amount of attention is covering deep insecurity. She who constantly giggles inappropriately may be hiding deep grief that she doesn't want to face. The rigid, controlling, or domineering person is covering fear and insecurity, and so on. As Jesus pointed out, "You will know them by their fruits."[3] Even though Jesus was referring to false teachers, the same principle applies to our personal problems. The symptoms in our life—whether they are physical, behavioral, emotional, relational, or spiritual—are the fruit of a deeper root we keep referring to. Again, to be healed we need to get to the root cause and deal with that. It's not that we neglect the symptoms. Not at all. But it isn't sufficient to treat only symptoms; otherwise the problem will poke its ugly head up somewhere else.

Meeting legitimate needs

Also vital for healing and wholeness is the need to accept responsibility for ensuring that we get our personal and legitimate needs met in healthy ways; otherwise we may seek to get them met in unhealthy ways or get sick.

❏ *Relational needs*

Besides the basic need for food, clothing and shelter, everybody has a need for meaningful relationships. As God said at the beginning of human history, "It is not good for man to be alone. I will make a helper suitable for him."[4]

It may not be most desirable for many, but one doesn't have to be married or have romantic relationships to be healthy, but as research has shown, one can't live healthily without at least one or some healthy and meaningful relationships. Loneliness can take years off a person's life by causing any of a number of diseases including heart attacks.

At the same time, research has shown that married people live longer than separated, widowed, divorced, and single people (especially single men). Happily married people have stronger immune systems. Thus, if we are not married, we need to ensure that we get our relational needs met in healthy ways. Another reason I believe women live longer than men is that they are much more gregarious than men and, as such, are much better at forming close relationships with other women than men are with other men.

A few years ago when I was single I had an intense pain in my left arm. I couldn't even put my car seat belt on without using both hands. I thought it may be caused or aggravated by my emotional state. I had just returned from overseas where I had been involved in a very intensive series of seminars and workshops. I had traveled and worked with a small team and felt unusually close to them as well as to many who attended our workshops. When I arrived home, besides being exhausted and struggling with jet lag, I missed the companionship and closeness of the people I had been with and was feeling let down, lonely, and depressed.

When I asked God to show me the cause of my pain, I realized that it may be caused or aggravated by my feeling disconnected from people I loved and who loved me. I spent the following weekend with a small group of understanding people and by noon on the first day the pain in my arm was gone.

We were created for relationships and cannot exist without them. But we need meaningful, healthy relationships because toxic or unhealthy relationships tend to promote unhealthy people. Relationships with such negative people, who are disconnected from their own reality, can literally make you sick. On the other hand, healthy relationships with loving companions help promote healing and help keep you healthy.

❏ *Physical needs*

Another contributing factor to many ills is a failure to take adequate and proper care of one's physical well-being. Essential for sustaining good health is the need for maintaining a healthy diet, regular exercise, and ensuring that one gets sufficient rest, relaxation, and sleep.

As there are many books and articles on this subject I won't go into detail. However, this is not to minimize the vital importance of taking care of one's body as an important factor in maintaining wellness.

❑ *Spiritual needs*

Of equal, or perhaps even more, importance is recognizing that we are not only physical and social beings, but also spiritual beings. For complete wellness we need not only a healthy relationship with ourselves and others, but also with God—a relationship we can have through his Son, Jesus Christ, who died for our sins and, in so doing, provided forgiveness for all our sins and made it possible for us to be reconnected to God and have a deep and meaningful relationship with him.

Karl Barth, the famous, though at times controversial, contemporary Swiss theologian, realized the importance of what Christ did for us so we could have a right relationship with God. Barth was a great thinker, a prolific writer, and had been a professor at several of Europe's leading universities. On one occasion he was confronted by a reporter who wanted a brief summary of his twelve thick volumes on church dogmatics. Barth could have given an impressive intellectual dissertation, but didn't. Quoting the popular children's hymn, he simply replied saying, "Jesus loves me this I know, for the Bible tells me so."

Knowing that God has forgiven us and cleansed us from our sins can give great peace of mind and free us from guilt—both of which are a part of and essential for total healing and wellness.

Regulating stress factors

Another requirement for healing and maintaining total wellness is regulating the stress factors in our life. Stress, in particular, is a killer and can take years off one's life. Dr. Joan Borysenko in her book, *Minding the Body, Mending the Mind*, says, "Recent major studies indicate that approximately seventy-five percent of visits to the doctor are either for illnesses that will ultimately get better by themselves or for disorders related to anxiety and stress."[5]

According to Dr. S.I. McMillen, author of *None of These Diseases*, the percentage of stress related illness is much higher. He writes, "Medical science recognizes that emotions such as fear, sorrow, envy, resentment and hatred are responsible for the majority of our sicknesses. Estimates vary from sixty percent to nearly one-hundred percent."[6]

❑ *Good stress, bad stress*

There are four types of stress. Only one is good. The pressure of an examination soon to be taken can motivate us to study in advance. If we don't, then we will experience bad stress. The need to eat, pay our bills on time, take care of our family needs are also good stress. These motivate us to work. Without good stress, many essential things wouldn't get done or worthwhile goals achieved.

❑ *Burning the candle at both ends*

I recall reading about a bridge with a ten-ton load limit built on a small country road that had operated successfully for many years over which multiplied thousands of vehicles had crossed—one or two at a time. Then one day a fifteen-ton truck tried to cross it and the bridge collapsed under the load. The second type of stress, which is bad or damaging stress, is caused by an overload of responsibilities all of which may be important. However, each one of us has his or her limit and can carry only so much weight before buckling at the knees and crumbling. Likewise, each one of us can handle only so many responsibilities and burdens without crumbling.

There comes a time when we need to say enough is enough, sort out our priorities, do what has to be done and let the rest go. We cannot continue burning the candle at both ends and expect to survive. It is not without good reason that one of the Ten Commandments given by Moses is to have one day a week for rest, meditation, worship, and spiritual renewal.[7]

❏ *Too much too soon*

A third stress—also bad stress—is caused by traumatic incidents, many of which are from circumstances out of our control. For instance, the death of a spouse or loved one, divorce, the loss of a job, a major change in life such as a new job, moving to a new area, and even buying a new home and taking out a large mortgage can all be very stress producing. Studies have shown that too many major changes within a given year can cause major sicknesses. When a major crisis happens, it is important not to make any unnecessary changes until the pain from the crisis is resolved.

❏ *Supercharged, repressed negative emotions*

The fourth type of stress—one of the most damaging of all —is caused by failing to resolve impaired relationships and the accompanying super-charged, repressed negative and damaged emotions. As John Powell pointed out, "When I repress my emotions, my stomach keeps score."[8] Or as the Godfather said in the film of the same name, "When the mind is stressed, the body cries out."

Any upset—large or small—can trigger these unresolved feelings, greatly magnify their effect, be extremely stressful, and produce intense anxiety. For example, "Fatal heart attacks can be triggered by 'anger in all degrees, depression, and anxiety,' according to Dr. Roy R. Grinker of the Michael Rees Hospital in Chicago. This doctor states that anxiety places more stress on the heart than any other stimulus."[9]

Unresolved and bad stress weakens the immune system and makes us much more susceptible to various ills. It also aggravates what sicknesses we already have. Someone has reminded us that the word "disease" comes from DIS-EASE, which in turn means ill-at-ease.

Other illnesses listed by Dr. McMillen that can be caused or aggravated by stress, anxiety, and worry include ulcers, rheumatic fever, coronary thrombosis, epilepsy, diabetes, obesity, hives, hay fever, asthma, back trouble, rheumatic arthritis, skin diseases, severe headaches, muscular pain, and many more. Constipation, diarrhea, various infections, hemorrhoids, eating disorders, frigidity and impotence, sexual and other addictions, and relational difficulties could also be added to this list.

❏ *You get the tiger or the tiger gets you*

As another has said, ongoing stress is like driving your car with one foot on the accelerator and the other foot on the brake. Or it can be likened to being chased by a tiger. It can cause you to be paralyzed by fear, to fight, or to run for your life. If you are paralyzed by fear, chances are you'll be eaten alive. If you fight for your life you may or may not win. If you run for your life, at least you'll burn up the excess adrenalin that pumps into your blood stream to prepare you for either fight or flight. When living under constant stress, the excess adrenalin will upset your body chemistry and in time will break down your health. Either you get the "stress tiger" or the tiger gets you.

❏ *What's inside is what comes out*

As adults it's not only what happens to us that makes us ill, but how we respond and react to what happens. And we always react on the basis of what's on the inside. Squeeze an orange hard enough and the juice comes out. The external pressure doesn't create the juice, it just exposes it. The same principle is true for us. Squeeze a person hard enough and what's inside comes out. If he has lots of anger within, he will either explode or implode. If he explodes, he may lash out and hurt others. On the other hand, if he implodes by turning his anger in on himself, he will eventually get sick.

The pressures of life and circumstances placed on us can add to our problems, but what increases their negative effect is that they trigger unresolved issues within. Two people can experience the same external stress; one gets his feelings out right away and doesn't lose a night's sleep while the other may fret and stew for days, weeks or even years, bottle up his feelings and become physically ill. It's what's on the inside—and how we learn to handle the emotions that stressful situations cause—that counts.

To choose or not to choose

To be healed and maintain good health and total wellness, we need to make this a conscious choice, and consistently apply and live by the principles for wellness that God has given us—principles that medical science has confirmed to be essential for total well-being.

Among these requirements is the need to identify and resolve the causes that make us sick, resolve any and all impaired relationships, ensure that our basic needs—physical, emotional, and spiritual—are met in healthy ways, and as much as is possible control the stress factors in our life that, if we don't, will make and keep us ill. To adhere to and apply these principles is a choice we all can make.

The good news is that, with God's help and other qualified help where needed, we can become much healthier and more loving persons if we make a conscious choice to be so, rather than leave our choices to chance. As another has said, "It is choice, not chance, that determines our destiny."

Footnotes:

1. Bernie S. Seigel, M.D., Love, Medicine & Miracles (New York: Harper and Row Publishers, Inc., 1986), 4.
2. James 5:16, (NIV).
3. Matthew 7:16 (NKJV).
4. Genesis 2:18, (NIV).
5. Joan Borysenko, Ph.D., Minding the Body, Mending the Mind (New York, Bantam Books, 1987), 3.
6. Dr. S. I. McMillen, None of These Diseases (Westwoood, New Jersey: Spire Books, Fleming H. Revell Company,1963), 7.
7. Deuteronomy 5:13-15.
8. John Powell, S.J., Why Am I Afraid to Tell You Who I Am? (Chicago, IL: Peacock Books, Argus Communications, 1969), 154.
9. McMillen, None of These Diseases, 62.

"Emotional illness is avoiding reality at any cost. Mental health is accepting reality at any cost."

5

Nothing Changes
If Nothing Changes

HAVE YOU EVER WATCHED a distraught parent in a supermarket trying to control an uncontrollable child? The kid is either grabbing at everything or throwing a tantrum and the mother says, "Stop!" which, interpreted by the child, seems to mean the opposite and achieves the opposite effect! Mother raises her voice. Junior cries. Mother gets angry and the angrier she gets, the louder junior cries—or screams! And the louder he gets, the more frustrated and mad mother gets!

Here's what's fascinating, the more of what mother does doesn't work, the more she does of it! That is, until she gives up her futile attempt to regain control of the situation and drags the child out of the store and shoves him into her car.

What parent among us hasn't had the same or a similar thing happen? For whatever reason when what we are doing with our children, spouse, or whoever doesn't work, we are inclined to do more of the same thing not realizing that (as the saying goes) "if we keep doing what we've always done, we'll keep getting what we've always got, and we'll keep feeling what we've always felt."

To keep doing the same thing and expect different results is one person's definition of insanity!

The point is, as another popular one-liner puts it: "Nothing changes if nothing changes." It should be obvious that if we want to bring about change in our life, improve our interpersonal relationships, and resolve our problems and sicknesses, we need to make some positive changes in our life. So where do we begin?

Perception versus reality

Besides changing the way we do some things, we also need to change our thinking, our attitude, and our beliefs. In reference to the latter, we don't always act consistently with what we profess, but we always act consistently with what we believe. For example, if we believe deep down that we are unlovable, we will act consistent with this belief and act unlovable towards others. In so acting we will set ourselves up to be rejected. This, in turn, will reinforce our belief that we are unlovable. If we believe deep down that we are bad, we will act badly. If we believe that we are a failure, we will set ourselves up to fail.

On the other hand, if we believe we are lovable, we will act in loving ways and receive loving responses. This, in turn, will reinforce our belief that we are lovable. Also, if we believe we are capable and successful, we will act accordingly and so on. A vital part of healing, therefore, is to change our attitudes and beliefs so they are in harmony with what we want to become and what we believe God wants us to be.

To change our belief system we need to change our view or perception of reality. As already stated, "We see things not the way they are but the way we are." Even though our perception of events may be distorted, that, to us, is our reality. However, until our reality about ourselves is in focus with what we actually are, there is little or no hope for change, healing or recovery. In other words, we need to be realistic and see ourselves as we truly are—the way God sees us! And then, little by little, we need to accept ourselves as we are—the same way God accepts us—warts and all. Until we do this, we are not free to change the characteristics that stop us becoming the person God wants us to be, which is complete and whole—fully alive and fully loving.

Facing reality is not a cure-all for every problem and sickness—such as an infection caused by tetanus, malaria caused by a mosquito bite, or a broken arm caused by a fall— but it is foundational for healing many physical symptoms, overcoming personal problems, resolving interpersonal conflicts, for enhancing our relationships, for emotional and spiritual healing, and for our total well-being.

Waving a magic wand and wishful thinking won't cure problems. Neither will any method that ignores the underlying causes of our problems. Such methods may relieve one symptom only to exchange it for another. Certainly, I believe in the power of prayer for healing but prayer divorced from one's reality is equally ineffective. There's no denying that the power of suggestion created by some prayer and certain "faith healers" can have a powerful effect on susceptible minds. Positive thinking, placebos, and some forms of religious hocus-pocus can have the same effect—but they don't cure the underlying cause of the problem. A witchdoctor's curse can be very powerful (in a negative sense) too. If people believe it, they can easily (unconsciously) cause the curse to happen.

Law one: The law of truth

When Jesus said, "You will know the truth and the truth will make you free,"[1] he gave us a principle as real and as universal as the law of gravity. We could call it the "law of truth" which, when heeded conscientiously, leads to freedom from spiritual, emotional, and many physical ills, as well as personal problems and relational conflicts.

The reverse side of the "law of truth" shows that while there is any area in our life where we haven't found freedom, to that degree we are still in denial; that is, there is some truth about ourselves that we are not seeing or confronting. Denial, as already noted, is possibly one of the most subtle and damaging sins of the saints! Lyman Coleman agrees. He wrote, "We are said to be a society dedicated, among other things, to the pursuit of truth. Yet, disclosure is often penalized. Impossible concepts of how men ought to be—which sadly enough are often handed down from the pulpit—make man so ashamed of his true being that he feels obliged to seem different ... yet, when a man is out of touch with reality, he will sicken and die; and no one can help him without access to the facts [truth]."[2]

Denial is a dangerous course to follow. If we don't see and accept what we are contributing to our ills, and blame others for the problems we have, we can damage or destroy our closest relationships. Furthermore, if we don't look at and resolve the character issues we are hiding, we can make ourselves ill—and take years off our life. In working in the area of divorce and grief recovery for the past decade or more, I think I could safely say that at least ninety percent of divorced people primarily blame their partner for their failed relationship. And as long as they stay in denial regarding the part they contributed in their relationship breakup and play the blame-game they will B-LAME; emotionally that is.

We don't have to be a religious Pharisee and hide behind a facade of external goodness or religiosity to be in denial and out of touch with our reality. Anything we use to hide behind to avoid facing our inner condition—whether it's religion, busyness, success, altruism, good works, sports, television, acting out in self-destructive behaviors such as alcoholism or any other addiction, or whatever—can be equally destructive.

Denial stops us seeing ourselves as we are on the inside. It stops us facing the root causes of our problems. It blocks our getting healed physically, emotionally, and spiritually. And it stops us finding true and lasting love—which, after all, is the highest fruit of maturity and wholeness.

Only when we see and admit that we are sick can we be healed. Only when we acknowledge that we are broken can we be fixed. Only when we see that we are not whole, can we be made whole.

The counterfeit versus the real

Unfortunately, when we don't have the real thing, we often settle for a counterfeit, which, at best, is a poor substitute and at worst, a disaster.

❏ *Lust versus love*

For example, lust is often mistaken for love. Initially, lust can look and feel like love, but it isn't love. Consequently, it can never satisfy the needs of the heart. Like alcohol or drugs, the one trying to fill his empty love tank through sex keeps doing more of the same in a vain attempt to find the love he hungers for which lust can never deliver.

❏ *Churchianity versus Christianity*

In the same way many have mistaken churchianity or religiosity for Christianity. It, too, can look and feel like the real thing but it isn't. Neither can it meet the need of the human spirit because it's not real, but a highly deceptive counterfeit that has led millions astray.

❏ *Works that don't work*

Personally speaking, for many years I did all the "right religious things" outwardly but still felt empty on the inside. I sought to anesthetize the pain of my emptiness by keeping busy, busy, busy—doing many good things. I thought I was being successful, but none of my good deeds ever made me feel good, loved, worthwhile, or accepted—nor did they satisfy the needs of my heart. I got lots of approval but by the end of the day I would feel just as empty as I did at the beginning of the day.

Getting to the Core

One day right out of the blue a simple but profound insight hit me: "The reason I feel empty is because I am!" To get in touch with and feel this emptiness connected me to a deeper level of my inner reality, and opened the door to the very core of where I needed the greatest measure of healing.

As long as I hid from and denied this painful part of me, I couldn't be healed. Only when I got in touch with this another broken part of me, felt its intensity, and owned it, could I begin to resolve it. Feeling the pain drove me to do something about it.

That's what God wants all our painful feelings to do—to draw us away from counterfeit and counter-productive experiences, and motivate us to seek the help we need for recovery. Feeling my inner emptiness also helped me to see that what I needed for healing was affirmation—not approval. While I knew intellectually that God loved and accepted me as I was, I needed to feel and experience his love and affirmation at the very core of my being—something I believe every person needs because our sin nature has not only left us broken but also disconnected us from God—the source of all love and life.

❏ *The power of affirmation*

Approval can never make us feel God's love and affirmation or anybody else's for that matter. There's nothing wrong with approval when it is given and received for the right reasons, but when it's used as a substitute for love to fill one's empty "love tank," it is never healthy or helpful. Besides that it doesn't work. Approval is based on what we do. Affirmation is based on who we are—regardless of what we have done or have failed to do!

Affirmation produces a healthy sense of self-love and self-worth, which is crucial for the healing of persons, for overcoming personal problems and negative behaviors, and for finding loving relationships. Without affirmation we will stumble along in the shadows of life never finding what the heart is yearning for.

Affirmation comes not only by being honest with ourselves and confessing our "dark side" (faults and sins) to God and receiving his forgiveness and acceptance, but also by confessing these same things to a safe and trusted friend or two. Through their not judging, condemning, preaching at, or making us feel bad, but loving and accepting us as we are—"warts and all"—little by little we learn to love and accept ourselves. Again, it is not without good reason that the Bible teaches us to confess our sins and faults to one another, for only to the degree that we are fully known can we be and feel fully loved. As we become known and accepted by loving people, we not only learn little by little to love and accept ourselves, but we also learn to feel closer to God and begin to sense his love and affirmation at the core of our being.

❏ *Martha, Martha, you are troubled about many things*

Recall the story of Jesus and his friendship with sisters

Mary and Martha. On one occasion when Jesus was visiting in their home, Mary sat on the floor at Jesus' feet and visited with him while Martha did all the work preparing the meal they were about to have. Martha got ticked off with Mary for not getting up and helping her. She said, "Lord, don't you care that my sister has left me to do the work by myself? Tell her to help me!" The way Martha saw the situation was reality to her, but it wasn't to Jesus! He saw things from a totally different perspective.

Jesus sided with Mary. He said something that Martha didn't understand, "Martha, Martha, you are troubled about many things. What you are doing is fine, but there is only one thing that is really important. Mary has discovered it."[4]

Like many of us, Martha was probably a workaholic—or a busyaholic—always keeping busy to avoid whatever it was that was troubling her. Furthermore, her feelings of worth were probably dependent on her performance. As already implied, performance may gain approval but such can never make one feel worthwhile, loved, or affirmed.

Jesus wasn't saying we shouldn't work. In fact, the Bible says that if a man doesn't work, he shouldn't eat.[5] What Jesus was saying to Martha, and to all of us, is that relationships are more important than performance. In fact life is relationships. It has been said that eighty percent of life's satisfaction comes from relationships. The opposite is also true. Most of life's unhappiness comes from poor or impaired relationships.

Martha was uptight because she wasn't facing the truth about herself. She was hiding her insecurities behind a facade of busyness and performance. Jesus called her on it because of the motive behind her "good works." True, she was a friend of Jesus and loved him, but was busy working in this instance because she was probably seeking his approval. Mary had chosen the better part in that she sat on the floor and related to Jesus. In so doing she experienced his affirmation without even looking for it.

As sick as our secrets

As they say in AA, "We are as sick as our secrets!" If, for example, one is hiding his fear of not feeling loved behind his busyness, and is driving himself too hard, or is a perfectionist seeking to prove to himself and others that he is an okay person, and happens to be a Type A workaholic, not only is he likely to have relational conflicts, but may develop serious heart problems. Francis McNutt explained: "Doctors Friedman and Rosenman wrote the ground-breaking *Type A Behavior and Your Heart*, about the connection they found between heart disease and the stressed out, irascible Type A personality. This knowledge has helped guide us (on the human level, at least) in knowing what to look for while praying for those with heart problems."[6]

Or if we are repressing negative thoughts and emotions, such as thoughts and feelings of failure, anxiety, rejection, jealousy, envy, bitterness, loneliness, guilt, shame, or fear and hiding behind a mask of intellectualism, authoritarianism, super sweetness, religiosity, super-spirituality, being a victim, or any of a score of other defense mechanisms, physical sickness and/or relational conflicts are often the result. Any of these can eat one's heart out, affect the body's chemistry, and weaken the immune system. Depression, too, is often the result of repressing and internalizing anger and other super-charged, repressed negative emotions.

It is true, "we are as sick as our secrets."

❏ *I was afraid so I hid*

The problem of hiding goes back to Adam. When he disobeyed God, he was afraid of being rejected so he hid or tried to hide from him. Mankind has been doing the same thing ever since. We not only try to hide from God, but also from other people for fear of their rejection. The danger in this is that if we do this long enough, eventually we hide from ourselves, and then no longer know who we really are. At that point—if it could be measured—one ceases to grow as a living person and begins to die. Instead of living fully, we are dying slowly without even knowing it.

To become fully alive again and be healed of our problems and sicknesses, we need to come out of hiding and face the truth about ourselves. There is no other way. Without access to the truth there is no healing, no growth, and no freedom.

M. Scott Peck put it this way, "Emotional illness is avoiding reality at any cost. Mental health is accepting reality at any cost."

Gerard Egan, in his book *Interpersonal Living,* points out that extensive discussions "based on both theory and research, indicate that people who cannot reveal themselves appropriately run the risk of impoverished lives and a wide variety of neurotic disorders."[7] Egan also quotes Sidney Jourard who affirms that every maladjusted person is one "who has not made himself known to another human being and in consequence does not know himself. Nor can he be himself. More than that, he struggles actively to avoid becoming known by another human being. He works at it ceaselessly, twenty-four hours daily, and it is work!"[8]

❏ *It's not the truth that hurts*

The basic fundamental need for growth and recovery is the need for relentlessly facing and accepting the truth about ourselves. Jesus didn't say, "You will know love and love will make you free." He said, "You will know the truth and the truth will make you free." Truth is not only the road to freedom it is the way to love. The truth that sets people free is not just the truth of God's Word, but the application of its truths to the "truth" or reality about ourselves.

Facing one's reality can be a painful process as most of us have spent years building walls around our inner self to protect us from further hurt. As somebody else has said, "It's not the truth that hurts but letting go of the lies!" For most of us, it's only when our pain is greater than our fear that we are willing and ready to break through our defenses and face reality.

The road to recovery

If you have difficulty seeing the truth about yourself, look at any symptoms you may have. Do you have any recurring physical problems? Any addictive or other destructive behavior patterns? Any recurring relational problems or impaired relationships? Or is there an emptiness in your life? If any of the above, ask God to help you trace your symptoms to their cause and lead you to the help you need to overcome, which may be through a trusted friend, a competent counselor, a support group, or all three.

More often than not it is a personal setback, an illness, a major crisis, a difficult situation, or a broken relationship that is God's wakeup call to motivate us to seek help and get into a recovery program.

❏ *No pretense*

"So get rid of your feelings of hatred. Don't just pretend to be good! Be done with dishonesty ... deception, envy, and fraud,"[9] is what the Apostle Peter wrote as a part of growing up into the fullness of our salvation.

In other words be real. If you are angry, hurt, sad or whatever, be honest about it. You don't have to lash out and hurt others with these feelings but simply state how you feel and learn how to express these emotions in healthy ways. The important thing is to be authentic. As Alan McGinnis says, "Psychologists disagree about almost everything, but on one point they display surprising unanimity: There is no such thing as a person who never gets angry—there are only those who suppress anger. And sending anger underground [and any other negative emotion] can produce a thousand psychosomatic problems, such as ulcers, migraines, and hypertension, and also some serious relational difficulties."[10]

The road to healing and wholeness starts at that point where we begin to be truthful with ourselves—especially with our emotions and motives—and face reality. Remember too that "nothing changes if nothing changes." So if you want to change your life for the better, be sure to embark on the "Truth Road" for it is the pathway to healing, recovery, and lasting love. Ask God to help you to do this. Today.

Footnotes:

1. John 8:32.
2. Walden Howard, comp., *Groups That Work* (Grand Rapids: Zondervan Publishing House, 1967), 23.
3. James 5:16.
4. See Luke 10:38-41.
5. 2 Thessalonians 3:10.
6. Francis McNutt, "Thoughts From Francis," *The Healing Line* (Jacksonville, FL: Christian Healing Ministries, Vol. 6, issue 9, June 1993) 1.
7. Gerard Egan, *Interpersonal Living* (Monterey, CA: Brooks/Cole Publishing Company, 1976), 40.
8. Ibid., 41, quoted from Sidney Jourard, *The Transparent Self*, 1971, 32-33.
9. 1 Peter 2:1-2, (TLB).
10. Alan Loy McGinnis, *The Friendship Factor* (Minneapolis: Augsburg Publishing House, 1979), 128.

"Becoming a Christian doesn't cure personality problems any more than becoming a Christian cures the common cold."

6

You Can't
Unring a Bell

ACCORDING TO DR. BRUCE NARRAMORE, Christian psychologist and founding dean of the Rosemead School of Psychology, who has counseled numerous Christian workers, missionaries and missionary children, "Every year more than seven thousand missionaries leave their field of service prematurely and at least 70 percent of those are for preventable reasons!"[1] Many of these missionaries and numerous other Christians are suffering from depression, personality disturbances, family conflicts, and other personal maladjustments.

It is over-simplifying to pass these problems off as the work of Satan as some want to do. As noted in an earlier chapter, it is true that Satan is the originator of all sin and suffering, and in some cases is directly responsible for personal problems, but blaming him for problems that are our responsibility will stop our understanding the cause/s of our difficulties and resolving them. Likewise, it is too simplistic to write off our problems as a lack of dedication to God.

There are multitudes of Christians who are deeply committed to God, but their dedication hasn't freed them from personality problems. Becoming a Christian doesn't cure personality problems any more than becoming a Christian cures the common cold.

Law two: The law of confession and repentance

One reason we don't resolve our problems is because we don't bring them into the open and talk about them. Talking about them isn't sufficient of itself, but after admitting to our self that we have a problem, talking to the right someone is vital for recovery.

Whether one's symptoms are of cancer or personal conflict, they need to be confronted and dealt with immediately. Many a life could have been saved had the symptoms of cancer been found and dealt with sooner. And many a missionary, minister, or layman could have been kept at his post had he admitted and dealt with his personal conflicts when symptoms first appeared. And many a broken or divorced home with its resulting suffering could have been saved had the early symptoms of conflict been admitted and the causes treated years earlier. We all have some problems. The sooner we admit having them, the greater the chance we have of resolving them.

"Get rid of all that is wrong in your life, both inside and outside,"[2] is what the scriptures advise. Repressing or denying problems is not getting rid of them; it will make their long-range effect much worse. To get rid of them we need to get them out in the open where they can be dealt with. In other words we need to confess them, not only to God but also to someone we trust—not to someone who will judge or condemn us—but to someone who will accept and support us, which brings us to the "second law" for healing and growth: The law of confession and repentance.

❏ *The foundation for healing*

I recently received an email message from a lady, whom I will call Enid, who desperately wanted healing from her relational conflicts and depression. In trying to convince herself, she argued that all she needed to do was confess her sins and problems to God. Understandably, she didn't want to confess to any other person because she had done this in the past and had been hurt badly. Undoubtedly she had confessed to the wrong person—to someone who wasn't safe and couldn't be trusted. I've done that, too, so I could appreciate her feelings. However, it is important not to allow what someone else did to us in the past stop us from pursuing the road to recovery in the present. What others have done to us is their issue. If we allow this to control us, that becomes another problem of ours.

Nevertheless, while confession to God is important to receive his forgiveness, confession to at least one other safe person is also essential for healing and recovery.

The Scriptures remind us that confession is foundational for healing. James writes, "Therefore confess your sins [and faults] to each other and pray for each other so that you may be healed."[3]

Em Griffin, author of *The Mind Changers*, wrote, "This is the most ignored bit of advice I know of in Scripture, probably because we're afraid that people won't like us or trust us when they see how crummy we really are. But the reverse is true. They've got the same sin problem. As we openly reveal our innermost struggles, the plastic masks we wear begin to slip. Human warmth escapes and people begin to respond in trust."[4] Not even God can help us until we admit and confess who and what we truly are. Only as we admit this are we open to receive his healing and begin to grow. Denial keeps us closed to all God has for us. Confession of itself is both freeing and healing. As Jesus said, "You will know the truth and the truth will make you free."[5] To fail to confess, such as hanging on to an unforgiving attitude, keeps us bound to the past.

❏ Spiritual well-being

Confession to God is needed for our spiritual well-being. Only as we acknowledge and confess that we are sinners in God's sight are we able to receive his forgiveness. The Bible says, "If we confess our sins, he is faithful and just and will forgive us our sins and purify us from all unrighteousness.[6]

❏ Emotional well-being

Confession is also needed for our emotional well-being. Wherever a problem is denied and super-charged negative emotions are repressed, we hurt ourselves and often our loved ones as well. These unconfessed sins, faults, and problems not only cause physical sickness and relational conflicts, but also emotional problems such as worry, anxiety, fear, guilt, and depression.

I recall when one of my sons was not quite four. He called me into his bedroom one night to tell me he couldn't sleep because he was angry. After he told me what he was angry about, I assured him that it was okay to be angry. Before asking him to tell me more about his feelings, I said to him, "Actually, I feel angry tonight too."

"What are you angry at?" he asked.

"I'd rather not say," I replied.

He then stated quite firmly, "Well, Daddy, I think you better tell me. You'll feel better if you do!" Out of the mouth of babes! He was right of course.

❏ *Physical well-being*

Third, confession is needed for our physical well-being. The needless suffering and sickness caused by unconfessed and unexpressed negative emotions, unconfessed sin, and unresolved guilt and grief would be impossible to measure. The anxiety, depression, and emotional *dis-eases* these cause, as repeatedly stated, lead to many physical diseases as well as to relational conflicts. Not only did the Bible teach this hundreds of years ago, but modern research has confirmed it. "Studies at the University of Rochester School of Medicine showed that depression tends to lower physical resistance to virtually every form of disease or affliction and makes you appreciably more susceptible."[7]

David, the psalmist, knew the high price of keeping secrets. He discovered long before Alcoholics Anonymous that "people are as sick as their secrets." He wrote, "There was a time when I wouldn't admit what a sinner I was. But my dishonesty made me miserable and filled my days with frustration. All day and all night your hand was heavy on me. My strength evaporated like water on a sunny day until I finally admitted all my sins to you and stopped trying to hide them. I said to myself, 'I will confess them to the Lord.' And you forgave me! All my guilt is gone."[8]

As David and so many others have learned—it isn't the truth that hurts us but letting go of the lies! What hurts us is breaking through the self-protective barriers we build around our inner self in order to cope. As a child we needed these to survive, but as an adult to fully live and fully love we need to break through these barriers to get to the truth of who we really are so we can resolve the issues that are the root cause of so many of our conflicts and ills.

Whatever we have ever done or have failed to do, and wherever we have been hurt, rejected, abused, and sinned against —all that has made us feel bad or ill—needs to be confronted and dealt with. What happened, happened! We can't take these things back any more than we can unring a bell. However, while we can't undo the past, we can confront and resolve it.

As the Bible teaches, as medical science has confirmed, and as personal experience has shown us, in the words of Rene Dubos: "What happens in the mind of man is always reflected in the disease of his body."

When King David committed adultery with Bathsheba, the wife of one of his top soldiers, and discovered he had made her pregnant, he did everything he could to cover his tracks and hide his sin. He attempted to get Uriah, her husband, to make love to her so it would look like he was the father of the child. When this failed, he made sure Uriah was killed in battle so he could then marry Bathsheba and in this way cover what he had done.

❏ *Nothing is hidden*

There were three things David overlooked, however:

First, the mind—both his conscious and unconscious mind—never forgets anything of significance, good or bad.

Second, guilt never goes away unless it is confessed and resolved; and

Third, no matter how well we think we have covered our tracks, nothing is hidden from God. He informed Nathan the prophet about David's sin and Nathan confronted David with it.

The burden of guilt David was carrying is reflected in his words, "My health is broken beneath my sins ... because of my sins I am bent and racked with pain ... my whole body is diseased."[9]

After he poured out his heart in genuine confession to God and asked for mercy and forgiveness for what he had done, he was able to write, "What happiness for those whose guilt has been forgiven! What joys when sins are covered over! What relief for those who have confessed their sins and

God has cleared their record. There was a time when I wouldn't admit what a sinner I was. But my dishonesty made me miserable and filled my days with frustration. All day and 'all night your hand was heavy on me. My strength evaporated like water on a sunny day until I finally admitted all my sins to you and stopped trying to hide them. I said to myself, 'I will confess them to the Lord.' And you forgave me! All my guilt is gone."[10]

❏ Choosing prison to end twenty-three years of hiding

Some time ago on the front page of our local newspaper was the photo with the heading, "Out of hiding." The caption beneath the photo read: "Handcuffed and smiling, Katherine Power, forty-four, is led into court in Boston. Her surrender ended twenty-three years of hiding after, as an anti-war activist, she allegedly drove the getaway car in a bank robbery in which a policeman was killed."[11] Facing the truth and going to prison was apparently more desirable to Power than continuing the lie she had been living for all these years, so she turned herself in to the authorities. She had been "a fugitive who spent fourteen years on the FBI most-wanted list until investigators declared the case unsolved."

A friend said, "She reached a point in her life that she felt she needed to be truthful with the people that she knew. She wanted to reconnect with her family."[12]

Not many would have the same background as Katherine Power had, but everybody has a secret or two that he or she needs to bring out of hiding. Every one of us therefore needs at least one trusted, safe person we can confess to in order to open the door to healing and freedom.

❏ The many faces of sin

Unfortunately, there is a tendency to think of sins mostly as negative acts such as cheating, lying, stealing, committing murder, adultery, idolatry, etc. However, according to the Scriptures there are at least three categories of sin.

First, there are the above sins which are transgressions or breaking of God's laws, including his Ten Commandments.

Second, are sins of rebellion where a person does his own thing whether God approves or not. Carried to its extreme, these sins have their roots in a person's belief that he is his own authority on what is right or wrong. In other words he puts himself in the place of God.

Third. This category of sin is much harder to understand and come to terms with. It is where we fall short of the standard of God—the standard of perfection and wholeness he planned for us. As the Apostle Paul put it, "All have sinned and fall short of the glory [or standard] of God."[13]

Sins of omission would come under this category. These are sins not of what we have done but what we have failed to do. As James said, "Anyone who knows to do good, and doesn't do it, sins."[14]

Also belonging to this category are the much harder to identify sins of the spirit. These include things like jealousy, envy, anger, resentment, hostility, grudges, guilt, shame, mixed motives, self-righteousness, emotional dishonesty, worry, anxiety, and all unresolved negative emotions.

❑ *Where we've been sinned against*

Many of the previous mentioned sins have been caused not only by what we have done, but also by what has been done to us; that is, where we have been sinned against. These are the hurts that caused us to be angry, hurt, bitter, resentful, fearful and so on in the first place. Unresolved, they cause innumerable physical sicknesses and relational conflicts. Furthermore, all of these issues from the past that we have failed to resolve, we bring into all our present relationships and contaminate them. To be set free it is critical that we confess these feelings as well.

These are the inner sins and faults that keep us bound and lead to physical, emotional, and relational pains. We may not identify many of these in ourselves but God does. As Samuel wrote, "Man looks on the outward appearance, but God looks on the heart—he sees a person's thoughts, feelings, and motives."[15]

❑ *The toughest sin of all to see in ourselves*

Even harder to identify and perhaps one of the most destructive, most common, and most seemingly innocent sins of all is the sin of denial—denying who we truly are, denying what we truly feel, and denying what our true motives are. Also, it is just as big a sin to lie to our self as it is to lie to someone else.

One of the major reasons God is opposed to all categories of sin is because sin is so totally destructive of human personality. Sin destroys that which God loves—us! It not only leads to eternal death and separation from God, the author of all love and life, but is the original cause behind every human conflict, physical and emotional sicknesses, sorrow and suffering.

❑ *Catharsis—an emptying out*

True confession is much more than a casual admitting of who we are and what we have done. The psychological equivalent of confession is catharsis, which means emptying out. Holding our secrets in is what makes us sick. Emptying them out—along with all the emotions that are bottled up with the secrets—makes us well. If all we ever do is talk about our problems, we can get stuck in them forever, and actually reinforce them for "what the mind dwells on the body acts on." We need to empty out all our negative emotions of anger, hurt, grief, loss, and terror so we can let go of our problems, be healed, and put them behind us.

❏ *Confession without repentance is a game*

Furthermore, the kind of confession or "emptying out" we're talking about is not bragging or grandstanding about our "sins" in order to get attention—or to see who has the greatest war stories—but being genuinely sorry and repentant. Confession without repentance—that is, confession without changing our ways—is a game. True confession begins at the point of embarrassment and implies that, with God's help and the support of loving friends, we determine to change our ways and do what we need to do in order to recover and get well.

King Solomon, one of the wisest men of antiquity, said, "A man who refuses to admit his mistakes can never be successful. But if he confesses and forsakes them, he gets another chance."[16] He also finds freedom, forgiveness, healing, growth, and recovery. Adhering to the "law of confession" is essential for all of these.

Footnotes:

1. Bruce Narramore, Project letter, Narramore Christian Foundation, Arcadia, CA, March, 2004.
2. James 1:21, (TLB).
3. James 5:16, (NIV).
4. Em Griffin, *The Mind Changers* (Wheaton, IL: Tyndale House Publishers, Inc., 1976), 131.
5. John 8:32.
6. 1 John 1:9, (NIV).
7. John E. Gibson, "What Has Science Learned About Anger," *Eastman's Modern Secretary*, September 1972, 11.

8. Psalm 32:3-5, (TLB)
9. Psalm 38:3, 6-7, (TLB).
10. Psalm 32:1-5, (TLB).
11. *Daily Bulletin*, Thursday, September 16, 1993.
12. Ibid., 4.
13. Romans 3:23, (NIV).
14. James 4:17.
15. 1 Samuel 16:7, (Paraphrase).
16. Proverbs 28:13, (TLB).

*"Whatever hurts we fail
to resolve from the past
we bring into our present
relationships and will either
hurt, contaminate or
destroy these relationships."*

7

The Magic Number: Seventy Times Seven

DURING A VISIT TO Yellowstone Park one writer observed that the only animal that the grizzly bear would share his food with was a skunk. It wasn't that the grizzly wanted to share his food but rather that he chose to. With one swing of his powerful paw he could have crushed the skunk.

I noticed a similar thing with humming birds at the feeder I used to have hanging on my patio. Tiny wasps took a liking to this feeder too, and I was rather amused at how these tiny creatures aggressively chased the humming birds away. The birds seemed rather aggravated but I never saw any of them try to chase the wasps away. They knew to leave them well alone.

So why did the bear allow the skunk to eat with him, and why do humming birds allow wasps to take over what is rightfully theirs?

Because they knew the high cost of getting even. Undoubtedly they've learned the hard way. Strange that we humans aren't as smart. Too often when we've been hurt, we want to get even. Sometimes we carry grudges for years, often repressing them from conscious memory, and end up hurting ourselves more than the ones we would like to get even with. We fail to see how damaging an unforgiving spirit can be, which brings us to our third principle for healing, the law of forgiveness.

Law three: The law of forgiveness

Nursing a long-standing grudge is not only a block to healing, it is a cause of sickness, whereas forgiveness is a healing agent. In failing to forgive someone who has hurt me, I can literally make myself sick. As another has said, "Failing to forgive is like drinking poison and waiting for the other person to die."

❏ *Whom do we forgive?*

Acclaimed motivational speaker, Brian Tracy, says that fifty percent of the adult population is still nursing unresolved anger and resentment towards their parents. If we are to find healing, not only physical, but also emotional and spiritual, it is critical to face and resolve our anger towards our parents and forgive them—and, as Tracy says, the other person we need to forgive is everybody else.

If we don't, we will pay a high price. I read about one astonished patient who was told by his doctor: "If you don't cut out your resentments, I may have to cut out a part of your intestinal tract."

Fortunately the man took the doctor's advice. He had been nursing a bitter grudge against a former business partner. He went to see this man, resolved their differences, and forgave him. When he returned to the doctor, his physical condition had cleared up.

Interestingly, medical science is finally catching up with what Jesus taught two thousand years ago and what the Old Testament part of the Bible taught three thousand years ago—that emotions such as fear, anxiety, worry, envy, jealousy, resentment, anger, and hatred are responsible for either causing or greatly aggravating many of our sicknesses, for damaging our relationships, and for holding us back in life.

❏ Forgive to be forgiven

Jesus pointed out another disturbing truth about an unforgiving spirit when he said, "If you forgive men when they sin against you, your heavenly Father will also forgive you. But if you do not forgive men their sins, your Father will not forgive your sins."[1] Again Jesus said, "And when you stand praying, if you hold anything against anyone, forgive him, so that your Father in heaven may forgive you your sins."[2] "Do not take revenge, my friends, but leave room for God's wrath, for it is written: 'It is mine to avenge; I will repay,' says the Lord."[3]

Judgment is best left to God. That's his responsibility. He is the only one in a position to do so fairly and justly. I believe what Christ meant was that an unforgiving spirit on our part is a sure sign that we haven't truly shown remorse to God for all our failures nor experienced fully his forgiveness.

Some of us may need to first experience God's forgiveness before we can truly forgive another because our own sense of self-righteousness or self-justification causes us to see another's faults without seeing our own. On the other hand, others may need to forgive someone who has hurt them before they are able to experience God's forgiveness. Whatever we need to do first may depend on our particular circumstances and perhaps our personality. The important thing to realize is that there are four aspects of forgiveness needed:

First, I need to seek forgiveness for myself for where I have hurt others.

Second, I need to forgive all who have hurt me.

Third, I need to understand that forgiveness is more often than not a process rather than a single event.

Fourth, I need to experience God's forgiveness for my sins and failures.

Forgiveness for where I have hurt others

Three of the hardest sentences to say in the English language are three of the shortest. Without the willingness to say these three sentences, and genuinely mean them, one's relationships will probably be a disaster and his physical health not much better. These words take only a few seconds to say but have the power to heal, the power to keep love alive, and the power to transform a life.

They are: "I am sorry. I was wrong. Please forgive me."

As already pointed out, unresolved guilt for the things we have done wrong, and for how we have hurt others, can be just as damaging in the long run to one's health and well-being as unresolved anger is towards others who have hurt us. The truth is that while most of us have been hurt at some time or another by someone close to us, many, if not most of us, have also done our share of hurting and need forgiveness not only from God but from those we have hurt.

Jesus himself stressed the importance of putting things right with an offended brother or friend when he said, "Therefore, if you are offering your gift at the altar and there remember that your brother has something against you, leave your gift there in front of the altar. First go and be reconciled [apologize to] to your brother; then come and offer your gift [to God]."[4]

There's no guarantee that our offended brother will forgive us, but we are to apologize, make amends, and seek his forgiveness wherever possible.

Forgiveness of others who have hurt us

It makes sense that if I want to receive forgiveness from those whom I have hurt, I need to be willing to forgive those who have hurt me. This can be extremely difficult if we have been hurt deeply. But it is possible.

❑ *Seventy times seven*

When Jesus encouraged us to "forgive seventy-times seven,"[5] he was thinking of our physical as much as our spiritual well-being. As Dr. McMillen says, he knew that a forgiving spirit would save us from "ulcerative colitis, toxic goiters, high blood pressure, and scores of other diseases"[6] which would include ulcers, asthma, arthritis, and heart ailments.

Jesus also said, "If your brother sins, rebuke him, and if he repents, forgive him. If he sins against you seven times in a day, and seven times comes back to you and says, 'I repent,' forgive him."[7]

This doesn't mean that we let people walk over us and deliberately hurt us. Not at all. Proverbs says, "A prudent man sees danger and takes refuge, but the simple keep going and suffer for it."[8] If people insist on hurting us and taking their anger out on us and are not repentant, we need to distance or separate ourselves from them. Nowhere does it say that we are to allow toxic people to dump their poison on us. Even then, if we do separate from toxic people, for our own sake we need to forgive them.

❑ *We don't have to like everybody*

Fortunately, God hasn't commanded us to like everybody. That would be impossible. But we are commanded to love people. Among other things this, at times, will mean tough love; that is, we do the most loving thing for others—keeping in mind that it is not loving to allow others to disrespect our boundaries and walk over us. The most loving thing we can do to "boundary-busters" is to not allow them to treat us in an unkind or unloving way even if this means we need to separate from them. The reality of life is that we can't trust everybody to be loving and kind or not to be mean and cruel.

Jesus didn't trust himself to everybody either, even those who wanted to follow him because of the miracles he did. John wrote, "But Jesus didn't trust them, for he knew mankind to the core. No one needed to tell him how changeable human nature is!"[9]

Confrontation is needed for boundary-busters. But even for these it is important that we don't hold a grudge against them. If we do, we end up hurting ourselves more than we hurt them.

"The advice of the Great Physician appears to have percolated even into the hard-boiled bulletin of one police department: 'If selfish people try to take advantage of you, cross them off your list, but don't try to get even. When you try to get even, you hurt yourself more than you hurt the other fellow.'"[10]

❏ *Free from the past*

In an article some time ago in *Time* magazine inspired by Pope John Paul's forgiveness of his would-be assassin, Mehmet Ali Agca, journalist Lance Morrow says that "the psychological case for forgiveness is overwhelmingly persuasive. Not to forgive is to be imprisoned by the past, by old grievances that do not permit life to proceed with new business.

"Not to forgive is to yield oneself to another's control. If one does not forgive, then one is controlled by the other's initiatives and is locked into a sequence of act and response, of outrage and revenge, tit for tat, escalating always. The present is endlessly overwhelmed and devoured by the past."[11]

❏ *A wall of resentment*

Furthermore, an unforgiving attitude is destructive to personal relationships. Sad to say, far too many close relationships, especially marriage and family relationships, are destroyed not so much by what has been done but by what hasn't been done—forgiving one another.

Whenever I fail to forgive my brother, a wall of resentment builds up between us and eventually we become estranged. But once I forgive him for his offense towards me, we can become close again and feelings of love are restored. At least I have done my part in bridging the gap between us in order to become close again. I can't change his attitude, but my forgiving attitude opens the door for him to respond in like manner and makes it easier for him should he choose to so do.

Forgiveness, however, needs to be genuine and not just a religious or sentimental act because it is "the right thing to do." If our forgiveness isn't genuine, resentment will poke its ugly head out at the most unexpected times—like when a couple get into an argument and drag up events from five, ten, and even fifteen years ago that they still feel resentful about. Obviously those things haven't been forgiven. Forgiveness may not forget the past but it lets go of it. Whatever hurts we fail to resolve—be it from yesterday or all the way back to early childhood—we bring into our present relationships and will either hurt, contaminate, or destroy these relationships.

Third: Forgiveness is a process

Forgiveness, however, doesn't happen overnight. It is a process. As already stated, a broken bone can heal in six weeks. Deeply hurt feelings usually take much longer to heal. The following steps are a vital part of the forgiveness process:

❑ *Admission*

"This just couldn't happen to me. It isn't real. It's all a nightmare. Everything will be fine in the morning," is a common and normal response to tragic and painful events. However, the sooner reality is faced the sooner one can begin to forgive and heal.

For years Joan refused to face the reality of her situation. She had been married for twenty-seven years when she finally walked out. It had been painful to admit that John no longer loved her. For years she excused his verbal abuse and physical violence by telling herself he won't do this again. "It must be my fault. I haven't been a good enough wife."

Joan had been hurt deeply but had refused to admit even to herself what John was doing to her. Her denial was slowly destroying her health and believing his lies was decimating her sense of self-worth. She had every right to be hurt and angry but instead of admitting it, she denied it and turned it underground.

Only when we admit we have been hurt, can we move towards forgiveness and resolution. Only the truth will set us free.

❑ *Confrontation*

According to author and counselor, Jeenie Gordon, a person cannot "heal or forgive until he has confronted the person who brought about the pain.

"When I was a passive person," Jeenie said, "I swallowed anger and pretended everything was okay. The dishonesty sent the pain underground, but eventually, anger erupted. It came oozing out in snide remarks, criticism, and sarcasm. From that dark pit, forgiveness cannot come."[12]

I have found the same principle to be true in my own experience. If I feel that a person who is important to me has done something to hurt my feelings, the sooner I confront him or her, the better I feel. I never find this easy, but as long as I nurse my hurt and anger, the more it builds a wall between us. Closeness cannot be maintained whenever I deny my hurt or when I refuse to be honest with my feelings. This doesn't mean that we attack the other person or necessarily blame him or her for our feelings. It means we need to tell them how we feel using "I" statements rather than "you" statements.

For example, "I feel angry and/or hurt about such and such and need to talk it over with you. I may be overreacting but I didn't appreciate what you did."

To resolve our hurt and anger, we need to be totally honest and admit exactly how we feel. Then we need to get these feelings off our chest—not by lashing out and hurting the other person, but by "speaking the truth in love,"[13] or by writing out our feelings until they are completely dissipated.

In situations where it is either impossible or unwise to confront a particular person, one can write to this person and ventilate his feelings—and then tear up the letter. If you do write out your feelings to such and such a person and feel you need to send the letter, I strongly urge that you never ... never ... never send the first draft. To get feelings out may take several drafts. Mailed letters need to be very carefully written and the truth always "spoken" in love.

To forgive another is not to ignore justice. Pope John Paul forgave his would-be assassin, but the man stayed in prison, and rightly so. And where we want others to forgive us, if we are genuine, we will want to do all in our power to make a just restitution. To oversimplify it, if I stole my neighbor's lawnmower, it isn't enough to admit to him that I stole his lawnmower and ask for his forgiveness. I need to return his lawnmower in at least as good a condition (preferably in better condition) as it was when I stole it.

❏ *Choice*

Being realistic, it's one thing to forgive those who have hurt us if they say they are sorry, but what if, when we have confronted them, they won't admit they have hurt us or don't even feel they have wronged us? It's even harder if they don't care that they have hurt us or have hurt us on purpose. How can we forgive these people?

According to one author, Susan Jacoby, we can't. She feels that "real forgiveness cannot take place without an acknowledgment of wrongdoing on the part of the person who is chiefly responsible for causing pain."[14]

If this is so, some of us are going to carry grudges for a long time. For example, Jim is one man who, if he waits for his daughter to come to him to say she is sorry, may never resolve his hurt and anger. His daughter, now an adult, has rejected him since he and her mother separated when she was a child. He has made many efforts to resolve their relationship but all to no avail. She's still blaming him for her parents' divorce even though her mother was involved with another man at the time, and she was the one who walked out on her father.

Jim's feelings of hurt and anger are understandable, but as long as he holds on to them, his daughter still has a hold on him. Not only are his hurt and angry feelings keeping him miserable, but they contaminate every other close relationship he has. Unless he resolves his feelings and forgives his daughter, they will keep him miserable and may ruin his health. Chances are, though there's no guarantee, forgiving his daughter could pave the way for her return. It would certainly make it easier for her.

True, when a person acknowledges his wrongdoing, it makes forgiveness much easier. But when he doesn't—which is often the case—forgiveness still becomes a choice.

❏ *Reconciliation*

Forgiveness and reconciliation are two different things. We are required to forgive but reconciliation isn't always possible. If we want to be reconciled to the person who hurt us, the same desire and mutual response on their part is needed. They too need to acknowledge what they have done and seek our forgiveness. This is always the ideal but it often doesn't work that way.

Fortunately, reconciliation isn't needed for our healing. Only forgiveness on our part is. Neither are we required to forget. What we need to do is to make reconciliation our goal and always strive to do our best to achieve this goal, but forgive regardless of the other's response.

❏ *Letting go*

It is essential to realize that forgiveness is impossible until we resolve and let go of the resentment we hold towards the one who has wronged us. Resentment is a mixture of hurt and anger and unless we resolve these negative emotions, we will continue to carry a grudge towards the one who hurt us. Therefore, to truly forgive, we need to resolve our hurt and anger.

Unless we do this, even though we say we have forgiven the offending party, there is a danger in repressing these emotions where, in the long run, they will harm our health, deaden our joy, and adversely affect all our present and future relationships. We cannot put forgiveness on top of unresolved hurt and anger. That would be like putting a Band-Aid over an infected sore without cleaning out the impurities in the sore. It's these unresolved negative emotions that stop our truly forgiving and letting go of our past hurts. Once the negative emotions are resolved, forgiveness is not only made possible, but becomes relatively simple if one chooses to forgive.

❑ *Time*

How long does it take to resolve these negative feelings? Until they have all gone; that is, until we aren't crying or angry anymore over what happened to us.

Only then can we let go of the past and be freed to forgive and get on with our lives, unencumbered by past hurtful experiences. However, it has been said that time heals all wounds. Unfortunately, this isn't so. Some people have been stuck in their resentment for years because they have never worked through the healing process. It's the process that takes time. Healing is the result of the process.

I have read that after a divorce, for instance, it can take one year of recovery for every five years a person was married. I can't verify this, but "Statistics remind us that eighty-five percent of divorced men and seventy-six percent of divorced women marry within fourteen months of their divorce. Those who marry within twelve months or sooner have a seventy percent chance of being divorced again! Even those who wait longer have a fifty-five percent chance of being divorced again."[15]

Whatever the cause of the pain, give yourself time to work through the healing process and to heal. Generally speaking, the greater the loss and pain, the greater amount of time it takes to heal. Whatever you do, don't look to romance to heal your wounds for that will be just another Band-Aid to cover your pain.

In fact, if every person resolved his/her personal issues before they were married, divorce statistics would diminish dramatically. Failing to do this is one of the major causes of marital and relational failure. This is because each partner brings his and her unresolved baggage from the past into every relationship.

Fourth: Forgiveness from God

To find complete healing, spiritual as well as emotional,

and peace of mind, we not only need to forgive all who have hurt us, but we also need to experience God's forgiveness.

There isn't a person alive who doesn't have some sins, faults and wrongdoing to confess and resolve, and who doesn't need God's forgiveness. As God's Word says, "If we claim to be without sin, we deceive ourselves and the truth is not in us."[16]

When God forgives us, he doesn't overlook his divine justice, but does so on the basis of his divine love. His justice requires a just sentence, which is spiritual or eternal death —which is being separated forever from God, the author of all love and life. But herein is the love of God expressed—in that he paid the price to meet the demands of his justice when he gave his Son, the Lord Jesus Christ, to die on the cross in our place as the just retribution for our sins and wrongs. Therefore, God can freely forgive us and not in any way violate his divine justice. When we confess our sins to him, he grants us a complete pardon for all we have ever done wrong.

The important thing is that we respond to God's love by first acknowledging our sin and wrongdoing and asking for his forgiveness, and then accepting his pardon. His Word says, "If we confess our sins, he is faithful and just and will forgive us our sins and purify us from all unrighteousness."[17]

And then, in appreciation to God for his forgiveness of us, let us freely forgive others as we ourselves have been so freely forgiven. "Therefore, as God's chosen people ... clothe yourselves with compassion, kindness, humility, gentleness, and patience. Bear with each other and forgive whatever grievances you may have against one another. Forgive as the Lord forgave you."[18]

Forgiveness frees both the one who forgives and the one who has been forgiven (providing he/she accepts it).

Forgiving and forgiveness are central and foundational for healing—physical, emotional, and spiritual. Modern psychology agrees and is now emphasizing this crucial fact that the Bible taught three thousand years ago.

Footnotes:

1. Matthew 6:14-15, (NIV).
2. Mark 11:25, (NIV).
3. Romans 12:19, (NIV).
4. Matthew 5:23-24, (NIV).
5. Matthew 18:22
6. Dr. S.I.McMillen, None of These Diseases (Westwood, New Jersey: Spire Books, Fleming H. Revell Company, 1963), 71.
7. Luke 17:3-4, (NIV).
8. Proverbs 22:3, (NIV).
9. John 2:24-25, (TLB).
10. McMillen, None of These Diseases, 71.
11. Time, January 9, 1984.
12. Jeenie Gordon, Cementing the Torn Strands (Tarrytown, New York: Fleming H. Revell Company, 1991), 93.
13. Ephesians 4:15.
14. McCall's magazine, October 1983.
15. Dick Innes, How to Mend a Broken Heart (Arcadia, California: ACTS Communications, 1999), 55-56.
16. 1 John 1:8, (NIV).
17. 1 John 1:9, (NIV).
18. Colossians 3:12-13, (NIV).

"Oh God, don't let me die without having fully lived and fully loved."

8

Hurt People
Hurt People

INSPIRED BY THE PRAYER from John Powell's devotional book, *Through Seasons of the Heart*, I have adapted and added another prayer to my regular requests to God: "Oh God, don't let me die without having fully lived and fully loved."[1]

I know this can't happen as long as I have bitterness, resentment, or an unforgiving spirit, and haven't resolved, gotten rid of, and let go of hurts from the past.

We ended the previous chapter with the question, how do we resolve negative feelings so that in the process, we don't hurt or destroy somebody else—which leads us to our next principles for healing and recovery—the laws of resolution and retribution.

Universal laws to live by

Life teaches us that we are the sum total of our past

experiences and shows how these experiences—both positive and negative have programmed us for living in the present. Life also reminds us that nothing of significance is forgotten. If not remembered by the conscious mind, significant and traumatic experiences are recorded in the unconscious mind —never to be forgotten. If traumatic and painful experiences from the past are not resolved at the time of the actual happening—and the negative emotions caused by these experiences not expressed in healthy ways—they lay dormant (but very much alive) in the memory waiting to be triggered and expressed in the most unexpected time and manner. Furthermore, these supercharged repressed negative emotions can take years off one's life.

In other words, if we fail to resolve our past, we are destined to repeat it and to pay for it one way or another. If we don't take advantage of the law of resolution we will automatically suffer from the law of retribution.

Whether we agree with it or not, life is governed by laws—some of which are universal and all of which cannot be defied or broken without suffering the consequences of retribution. These laws are not to limit our life in any way but to make living life to the full possible. They are for the protection and good of all. Consider the following laws for example:

❏ *The law of gravity*

As we well know, the law of gravity says that what goes up comes down. It is a universal law and literally holds the universe together. It keeps my feet on good old terra firma (and the more firma the less terror). And it prevents all of us from flying off into outer space. It also rules that if I jump out of an airplane without a parachute, I will kill myself. Sure, I can defy and rebel against the law of gravity if I foolishly choose to, but it won't negate the law. If I defy and try to break it, it will break me.

❏ *The law of aerodynamics*

However, on the other hand, the law of aerodynamics makes it possible for birds to fly and airplanes to circle the globe. This law does not do away with the law of gravity but makes it possible to rise above it when strictly adhered to. If not strictly obeyed, the effect can be devastating. As the law of aerodynamics compensates for the law of gravity, so the law of resolution is provided to compensate or rise above the effects of the law of retribution.

❏ *The law of physics*

The law of physics says that for every action there is an equal and opposite reaction. If I light a fire, something is burned. Directed, the fire can cook my dinner, warm me in the winter, or power electric generators to light an entire city, and achieve endless good for mankind. However, if misdirected it can burn down that city, kill hundreds of people, and wreak havoc wherever it goes. Laws for living are the same. Adhered to they bring life and love. Disregarded they reap havoc and retribution.

Law four: The law of retribution

The law of retribution says that for every deed there is a consequence—either positive or negative. The word retribution itself means to pay back. As Webster says, it can be a deserved reward or punishment. If I eat, I live. If I don't, I die. If I connect to loving people, I will receive love. If I don't, I won't. Isolation and loneliness will be the payback. If I commit a crime, I will pay for it. If not caught by the authorities, I will pay for it through guilt. If the guilt is repressed and denied, chances are I will pay for it in my health or in some other adverse way. Sooner or later I pay. There is no escape. It's not that God punishes us. We punish ourselves.

For instance, the financial broker whom I trusted to take care of and invest wisely my retirement fund—my savings of thirty years—stole my entire fund and then blew, hid, or gambled every penny of it ... along with the funds of five other clients who also trusted him. Today, at the time of writing, he sits in jail and has cancer.

As certain as the law of gravity determines that what goes up comes down, so the law of retribution determines that what issues I fail to resolve and what negative emotions I don't get rid of, I will reap negative consequences for—not only through physical sickness, emotional illness, relational conflicts, and/or addictive and destructive behavior patterns; but also by projecting them onto other people—especially the ones I love the most. Some of these negative consequences are as follows:

❏ *Hurt people hurt people*

First of all, we need to realize that failing to resolve past issues is perhaps the single most destructive factor that breaks up families and close relationships. It doesn't make any difference whether you are a dedicated church member, devoted Christian, Jew or Catholic, a dignified Presbyterian, a staid Baptist, an upbeat Charismatic, a committed Mormon, Muslim or a disinterested atheist or agnostic. Hurt people hurt people. Period. And they keep on hurting people until they resolve their own hurt and pain.

If I don't resolve my anger at my boss, chances are that I will take it out at home either by kicking the cat or by being mean to or withdrawing from my family.

If a man was over controlled or smothered by his mother and is still angry at her, at the slightest provocation or misunderstanding he will overreact to his wife and other women and take his anger out on them. Or if a woman was mistreated by her father or other significant male and has never resolved her hurt and anger, she will take it out on her husband and other men.

It is a fact of life that loved people love people and hurt people hurt people. And the only way to stop hurting people is to resolve one's own hurt.

❏ Resolve it or repeat it

Second, what we don't resolve we are destined to repeat in one way or another. For example, an individual's behavior in the future can be best judged by his or her performance in the past.

Furthermore, children from divorced homes are more likely to be divorced than those from happy and loving homes. Many, if not most child molesters were themselves molested when they were children. And abused children often become abusing adults.

❏ What we project is what we get back

Another way the past is repeated is in the way we relate to other people. Basically, we treat ourselves the way we were treated and others treat us the way we treat ourselves. If we felt loved as a child, we will feel loved as an adult and attract loving people to us. If, on the other hand, we felt rejected as a child, we will feel rejected as an adult and attract rejecting people to us. In other words, if we hate ourselves we cannot believe that others love us, so unconsciously we set ourselves up to be rejected. What we feel about ourselves —good or bad—is what we project and what we project is what we get back.

❏ The sins of the fathers

Another way unresolved issues from the past are repeated is through the repetition of the mistakes of our family of origin. For instance, without resolution, the man who grew up with a controlling domineering mother is more likely to be attracted to and marry a woman who in some way, at least emotionally, is just like his mother.

Furthermore, if his marriage fails and he gets divorced and still hasn't resolved his mother issues, in all probability he will be attracted to the same type of woman again—and repeat the pattern. This is because he is unconsciously looking for the love he never received as a child. That is, he is still looking for a mother to love him and he wants to make it right this time—which of course doesn't and cannot work because romantic love is for adults, not for adults still looking for a child's mother love.

What is more, without resolution his children will be "programmed" to repeat the family history. They will tend to repeat the patterns of the way they learned to relate in the home they grew up in. This is what the Bible means when it says that "the sins of the fathers visit the fourth generation."[2] Perhaps more than anything else it is the "emotional sins" that get passed on from generation to generation. This affects women just as much it does men.

Just as domineering, controlling men tend to be attracted to weak, passive females, so domineering, controlling women tend to be attracted to weak, passive men. Both do this because controlling people have a neurotic need to be in control of their partners in order to feel safe. At the same time weak, passive partners have a neurotic need to be over-dependent on someone in order for them to feel safe. The problem is that domineering mothers tend to reproduce domineering daughters and passive sons, and domineering fathers tend to produce domineering sons and passive daughters (unless the daughter rebels against the domineering father and becomes domineering herself and is attracted to a man she can dominate.)

The reality is, while there is not a fixed rule, we parents don't always produce the children we want but the children that we the parents are. In one way or another our unresolved issues are passed onto our children, and as the Bible says, to the third and fourth generation—and the vicious cycle continues until someone says enough is enough and gets into recovery to break the chain from generations past.

Either we resolve our past or we are programmed to repeat it. The patterns of life always follow the programming. Always. Deprogramming through resolution is the only way to break the pattern.

❏ *Pass it back or pass it on*

Third, if we don't resolve our past and pass or direct our negative feelings back to where they belong, we will inevitably pass them on to where they don't belong. That is, we will take out our hurt and anger on those to whom it doesn't belong and who don't deserve it—often on the ones we love the most because they are the closest to us and with whom we feel the safest.

For example, a woman who was abused as a child by her father, grandfather, uncle or some other male, unless she directs that anger back to where it belongs and resolves it, she will inevitably take it out on her husband, sons, and/or other male figures.

The mother of one family I worked with had been badly sexually abused as a small child by a grandfather who threatened to kill her if ever she told anyone. At the time she was so terrorized that she buried all those fearful memories in order to survive. Unfortunately those feelings lay dormant and never went away. When she married, those ancient feelings were triggered. Physical touch to her was like being raped all over again. For many years she had projected the rage that belonged to her grandfather onto her husband, and later,

when her sons grew taller than her husband, she trans-
ferred much of her anger onto them as well. Unless she
places her anger back where it belongs—and resolves it—it is
highly unlikely that she will ever be able to relate in a healthy
manner to any adult male. Her marriage ended in divorce.
Sadly, this type of situation is repeated innumerable times
as so many children—boys as well as girls—have been sexually,
physically and/or emotionally abused.

It's the same with a man who had a poor or an abusive
relationship with his mother and hasn't resolved his issues.
He will inevitably take his negative feelings out on his wife,
daughters, and other women. If he doesn't do it overtly, he
will do it covertly through passive aggression, a negative
critical attitude, by being forgetful of the things that are
important to his wife, and by being hurtful to her, and so
on. In other words he will treat his wife as if she were his
mother and take out his frustrations on her. Unless he
resolves his mother issues, his marriage will be put to a
severe test and may not survive.

The reality is that we either resolve our past or we repeat
it and, in turn, pass it on in one form or another to our off-
spring.

Law five: The law of resolution

Fortunately in life, while there is always a negative for every
positive there is also a positive for every negative. Pain can
be turned into gain. Difficulties can be turned into learning experiences. Failures can be turned into stepping-
stones on the pathway to success, and problems can be
used as opportunities for growth. It's not so much aptitude
that makes this so, but attitude.

And as there is a law of retribution, there is a law of
resolution. My attitude will largely determine which law I

choose to abide by, and this in turn will determine my future. Here's how the law of resolution operates:

To heal it we need to feel it

To resolve and heal our pain from the past—be it feelings of hurt, anger, fear, grief or guilt—we need to feel it. If we don't feel it, there's no way we can resolve it. To feel it means we need to get connected to our past and recognize what our true feelings are. If we've been rejected, abused, abandoned, or mistreated unfairly we should feel hurt, angry, and afraid of being hurt again. These are the right feelings. If we don't feel anything, chances are our feelings are buried and repressed—an unhealthy course to cling to as an adult. If so, we may need the assistance of a trained counselor to help us get in touch with these damaging emotions.

Unfortunately, when we bury negative feelings we end up burying positive ones along with them. The walls we put around our heart to stop feeling our pain are not selective. They block feelings of love and other positive emotions as well.

It isn't enough to admit intellectually that we've been hurt, nor is it helpful just to talk about our feelings—doing this can keep us stuck in our pain and self-pity forever. We all know people who are nursing grudges and dwelling on and talking about hurts that happened years ago.

To resolve our past we need to get connected to our pain and feel it in all its intensity, which at times can be gut wrenching. The only way out of it is to go through it. Pain was the way into our problems. It is the way out of them. Thus, to heal it we need to feel it.

❏ *To feel it we need to relive it*

The next step to resolution is to relive the past hurtful experiences so we can get in touch with and connected to our pain. We need to go back in our memory and bring these past painful experiences into present consciousness. That is, bring them up onto the screen of our mind, see them happening again, and relive them. Easy? No, but essential, as this connects us to the pain so we can feel all the emotions that these experiences evoked at the time they happened. We then need to express these emotions in healthy ways as we were understandably not able to at the time the events occurred.

❏ *To relive it we need to get real about it*

It's these unresolved negative and damaged emotions that keep us stuck and stop our fully living and fully loving. To be free of these damaging emotions we need to be real about them so we can be rid of them. As the Bible so wisely advises: "So get rid of your feelings of hatred [anger]. Don't just pretend to be good."[3] And again, "If you are angry, don't sin by nursing your grudge. Don't let the sun go down with you still angry—get over it quickly; for when you are angry you give a mighty foothold to the devil."[4] This principle applies to all negative emotions. Buried they destroy us. Expressed creatively they heal us.

And what we didn't get rid of in the past we need to get rid of now. Wishful thinking doesn't take super-charged repressed negative emotions away. They just build up interest. The challenge is, how do we get rid of these destructive and damaging emotions? And how do we stop hurting so we will stop hurting other people?

To heal it we need to feel it. To feel it we need to relive it. To relive it we need to be real about it. And then, how do we get rid of it? We'll answer this question in the next two chapters.

Footnotes:

1. John Powell, S.J., *Through Seasons of the Heart* (Allen, Texas, Thomas More, 1987), 288.
2. Exodus 20:5, (Paraphrase).
3. 1 Peter 2:1, (TLB).
4. Ephesians 4:26-27, (TLB).

"As 'every unshed tear
is a prism through which
all of life's hurts are distorted,'
so every unresolved conflict is
a filter through which all of my
beliefs about life, myself, others,
friends, love, and about God
are distorted too."

9

Blessed Are They Who Mourn

I HAD JUST SPENT an entire week—day and night in an in-depth marathon workshop with a man I shall call Jack. At the close of the week Jack came to me and said, "Dick, I still feel you're not accepting me."

What do I say? Do I make up some phony excuse or do I tell Jack the truth? I decided on the latter.

"You're right, Jack," I said, "I'm not accepting you because I still have no idea who you are. Let me see the real you and I'll be the first to accept you."

"Fair enough," was his only reply and walked out of my life. I heard that he dropped out of our follow-up program, too. This man had a major abuse problem which he refused to face and resolve. He chose rather to hide behind a facade of superficial religiosity. The last I heard of him was that his wife divorced him.

Jack was a man who was a master at speaking "christian-eze." He could quote Bible verses, talk church language, and pray with all the right words. It was the kind of prayer that was like eating too much chocolate—sickly sweet.

He was a flat-line person in that he showed no feelings whatsoever. He just wasn't real. He had no idea why after twenty-five years of marriage his wife walked out on him. She was dying of loneliness. He couldn't understand why. Nothing she did could get him to open up and communicate what he was feeling. His feelings were repressed and shut off. Instead of living fully he was dying slowly. He was, as it were, an emotional time bomb ready to explode.

To fully live and fully love we need to understand emotions and how they affect every area of life. For instance, if like Jack we bury and build walls around our heart to block out our painful feelings, those same walls block out our positive feelings of love, joy, peace, wonder, and so on.

Feelings empower

Feelings or emotions are neither right nor wrong. It's what we do with them and how we handle them that counts. They are God-given and put sparkle into life. Without them, as another has said, "Life would be like playing a trombone with a stuck slide." Imagine how dull, boring, and monotonous that would be. In fact, people who bury and deny their emotions are characteristically bored with life.

Furthermore, without being in touch with and connected to one's emotions it is impossible to experience closeness and intimacy. Partners who never open up and share their feelings live together alone apart. If one hungers for intimacy and can't get this need met with his or her partner, he or she can become a candidate for loneliness, for despair, an affair, divorce, and/or a physical or emotional breakdown. Real people have real feelings and have a need for closeness, intimacy, a sense of belonging, and a legitimate need for someone they feel safe to share their feelings with, someone to listen to them, someone to care, someone "to be" with, and someone to be connected to.

To be is to be in relationship. However, without being connected to my emotions—my inner self—it isn't possible to be emotionally connected to any other person—or to God for that matter. One may know intellectually that he is connected to others and to God, but he won't be able to feel it, which causes his emotional and spiritual life to feel blah. Not that most people are totally disconnected from their emotions—although some are. Most of us probably fall somewhere in between both ends of the emotional spectrum. The more connected we are the healthier we will be. On the other hand, the more disconnected we are the more maladjusted we will be.

Keep in mind, too, that I can only be loved to the degree that I am known. And I can only be known to the degree that I am in touch with my inner self and my emotions.

Being connected to our emotions is what makes us real. It gives us strength. It empowers us. Also, to be Christ-like means to be connected, to be in touch with our total inner self and all of our God-given emotions. The person who can't feel is unreal. Unlike Nathanael of whom Jesus said when he first saw him, "Here comes an honest man,"[1] or as other translations put it, a man in whom there is no guile; that is, nothing false! Nathanael was open-faced. Jack, whom we wrote about earlier, was closed-faced, expressionless. His empty, lifeless eyes betrayed a very lonely and frightened man. He was disconnected and among the living-dead.

Being disconnected from our emotions makes us unreal. It takes away genuine strength and we end up in denial, with impaired relationships, being wishy-washy, weak and passive, or by becoming overtly aggressive, which is a poor substitute for and a counterfeit of true strength! A bully isn't strong. He's afraid and overcompensates by appearing to be tough. Underneath his facade is a frightened, hurt little boy. By pushing other people around, he thinks he is strong, not realizing that one of a man's greatest strengths is his gentleness—and having the ability to admit his weaknesses.

Being disconnected from feelings can also make us ill, take away our joy, and leave us empty and unfulfilled.

When David asked God for wisdom, he acknowledged that it was a matter of the heart, not just the head. And when the Bible speaks about the heart it includes the will, the intellect, and the emotions. Knowledge is left-brain, a matter of the "head." Wisdom is a balance between the thinking left brain and the feeling right brain. It is a balance between right-brain knowledge and left-brain intuition.

David prayed, "Surely you desire truth in the inner parts; you teach me wisdom in the inmost place."[2] And again, "Teach us to number our days aright, that we may gain a heart [not a head] of wisdom."[3]

Feelings are amoral

When parents, teachers, preachers, leaders or anybody else tell us we shouldn't feel hurt, that we shouldn't get angry, that we shouldn't express our emotions, or that we shouldn't feel the way we feel, they are wrong—dead wrong. We feel the way we feel—whether we should or shouldn't is beside the point.

By the time I was five years of age somehow I had learned that big men—real men—don't cry. This, of course, was typical of the culture in which I grew up at that time. The fallacy with this teaching is that a little boy of five is not a big man. Neither is it true that real men don't cry. It's men who are afraid to face and show their feelings that don't cry.

One of the great lessons we learn from the life of Jesus is that he never hid his feelings. When he was angry at the moneychangers in the temple who were ripping off the poor and grossly misusing the house of God, he turned their tables over and drove them out of the temple with a whip. While Jesus was meek, he never was weak. Regarding the phony religious Pharisees he condemned them and their actions in no uncertain terms. When he was weary, he rested. When he was lonely, he chose to be with friends. When he began his ministry, he chose the twelve disciples that "they might be with him." And when he grieved at the time of the death of his friend, Lazarus, he wept. Dare we do any less?

Not only did I learn that it wasn't okay to show my feelings—at least my negative feelings—later I learned that feelings couldn't be trusted. I learned early in life that denial was the only way to fit in and survive. But by the time I hit my early to mid thirties, I became very conscious of an inner emptiness that was beginning to plague me. To avoid this feeling and other deeply buried feelings I became a workaholic! Little did I know that my emptiness was a symptom and result of long forgotten, deeply buried, repressed negative emotions.

The good news is that my pain drove me into recovery. Since then I have learned that all my emotions are valid and that I can always trust my feelings. What I can't always trust is my interpretation of them. Learning to interpret feelings takes time and experience. The important thing to realize is that feelings are always valid. While we may not always be able to interpret them correctly, they are a thermometer, or an indicator letting us know what is going on inside of us.

Jesus never told us how to feel, only how to act. Feelings are amoral. As already noted, they are neither right nor wrong. It's what we do with them that counts. Furthermore, it's just as big a sin to deny our emotions, to bury them, and turn them in on one's self as it is to lash out and hurt somebody else with them. Emotions are meant to be expressed in creative ways. If they aren't, they will be acted out in destructive ways. Living as—or with—a repressed person who is in denial isn't living at all. It's eking out an empty existence. A person in denial can't be trusted because you never know for sure what is going on in their mind, and whether what they tell you is the truth or a lie. It can also be dangerous living with such a person because if they have hidden rage and it gets triggered, you can become the victim of their outbursts.

As an aside, I firmly believe that one of the major reasons for so much violence in today's society and among families is because so many people have never learned to resolve their hurts, disappointments, and anger in healthy ways. Their anger builds up and becomes hostility and/or rage and when it gets triggered, they lash out and take it out on anyone who happens to be in the way of their objectives.

Feelings are meant to be expressed

Imagine living in a world where we couldn't laugh at things that were funny or hilarious. We'd die, or as I like to kid, we'd blow our "foof-foo" valve! God gave us laughter to express our joy and hilarity. He also gave us tears to express our grief and sorrow—and he gave us a voice to express our terror and anger. If you go to a Disneyland type theme/fun park such as Magic Mountain and ride on the corkscrew Viper and you're scared out of your brain, it's perfectly normal—and acceptable—to scream your head off. What is more, it's expected. If you go to a football, soccer, basketball, or whatever game and your team is winning, you're allowed to get excited, cheer, and yell your head off. But in everyday life, while change is coming, too many of us were taught in childhood to stuff our feelings and act grown up! This has proven to be very unhealthy and damaging—not that I'm suggesting we jump up and down, cheer, and yell our head off when we go alone to the mail box and find an exciting letter! We can save the jumping-up-and-down until we get inside the house; otherwise the neighbors might think we are a little strange. While feelings are very important and need to be expressed, they do need to be expressed in an appropriate way at the appropriate time.

True, overreacting to emotions, expressing them in destructive ways, and allowing them to control us is childish (not child-like) and immature. However, acknowledging them and expressing them creatively in healthy ways is far from being childish and immature—it is an expression of healthy adulthood and maturity.

Sitting on and stuffing emotions, especially negative ones, isn't being in control of them. It is denying them, which places them in control of us. This is one of the major causes behind physical sickness and relational conflicts. The reality is if we don't control and express emotions creatively, they will control us in some self-destructive or other destructive way. What we fail to talk out creatively, we will inevitably act out destructively.

Sitting on positive emotions isn't the best idea either. Even the Bible says that, "Open rebuke is better than secret love."[4]

Being fully human and fully alive

To be fully human and fully alive is to be in touch with your total inner self—your inner reality—knowing not only what you are thinking but also what you are feeling. Without emotion there's no meaningful motion to life, no real meaning, and no zest for living. Furthermore, until we learn to feel with all our heart and to weep with all our heart, we will never know how to love with all our heart. We can't have one without the other.

So get rid of your negative feelings

As noted in the previous chapter, as a part of growing up the Apostle Peter not only said we need to "put away all evil, deception, envy, and fraud," but also to "get rid of our feelings of anger."[5] This principle equally applies to getting rid of all negative emotions.

When it comes to dealing with the past and emotions that have their roots in the past, some Christians like to quote the Bible verse that says, "Brothers, I do not consider myself yet to have taken hold of it. But one thing I do: Forgetting what is behind and straining toward what is ahead, I press on toward the goal to win the prize for which God has called me heavenward in Christ Jesus. All of us who are mature should take such a view of things."[6] Paul, of course, was referring to his "confidence in the flesh" which included his pride in being a Jewish Pharisee. This he put behind him.

The reality is, however, until we deal with the past and all the negative emotions associated with it, we can't forget it and put it behind us. Our unconscious mind won't let us. The biblical principal is to be honest with all our emotions, including those we have bottled up from past experiences, deal with and resolve them so we can let go of them and put the past behind us. Only then can we get on with living fully in the present and work toward achieving a worthwhile goal in the future. Besides, the Apostle Paul who said, "Forgetting what is behind," also warned about the danger of burying anger, not resolving it quickly, and nursing grudges![7]

Three choices

There are three possible avenues to take when dealing with emotions. We can suppress them, repress them, or express them—either creatively or destructively.

❏ *Suppression*

Suppressing emotions is being aware of what you are feeling but consciously holding the feelings in. This is sometimes necessary when it is not appropriate to share your feelings where and with whom you are. A possible setback with suppression, however, is that it can lead to repression.

❏ *Repression*

Repressing emotions, whether we are aware of what we are feeling or not, is stuffing them deep down inside so we no longer become aware of them. They get buried in the unconscious mind but, as already noted, never buried dead, but very much alive—never to be forgotten. Pardon the expression but the stuff we stuff, stuffs up our life and our relationships. With buried emotions we end up living in a state of denial.

❏ *Expression*

Expressing emotions is not only feeling them but dealing with them—either creatively or destructively.

Whenever possible, emotions are best expressed at the time they are felt or, if this isn't possible or appropriate at the time, they need to be expressed as soon as possible. It's best not to sit on them for too long as this can lead to repression. Only as they are expressed do we get rid of them. Obviously they need to be expressed creatively, not destructively.

For instance, we don't have the right to lash out and hurt others with our pent-up feelings, but it doesn't necessarily mean that we are going to be nice either. Consider Jesus' example again. He wasn't always "nice, proper, nor politically correct." When his friend Lazarus died, he didn't pretend everything was fine, because it wasn't. He acknowledged his loss and cried unashamedly.[8] That's what tears are for. And when Jesus was terrified on the eve of his crucifixion, he literally sweated it: "And being in anguish, he prayed more earnestly, and his sweat was like drops of blood falling to the ground."[9]

Before we know how to express and resolve negative emotions, we need to understand them and recognize them for what they are; that is, identify and know what you are feeling. Is it hurt, anger, fear, guilt, shame, anxiety, or a combination of any of these?

For some of us, as it was for me, identifying what I was feeling was like learning a whole new language—a strange, foreign language. And it took a lot of practice over time to get it.

Of all the varied emotions there are at least four major ones out of which associated feelings come. For instance, anxiety is a form of fear. Hate and resentment spring from unresolved anger. Sadness can come from grief, and so on.

When emotions are used and expressed as they are meant to be, each one is healthy and has a constructive purpose. When misused, they become unhealthy and destructive. Each has a good and a bad use.

Good anger, bad anger

❏ *Good anger*

When Jesus was angry, he didn't mince words. He felt it, acknowledged it, and expressed it precisely—both verbally and physically. When he was angry, he had a good reason to be, and did something about the situation that caused him to be angry. When he was angry at the money changers who were ripping off the poor in the temple, and drove them (the money changers) out with a whip, his anger was purposeful and directed. He used it to defend the defenseless and to bring about change—not to defend himself.[10]

That's what righteous anger is all about while, on the other hand, unrighteous anger or carnal hostility is all about one's own unjustified self-interest.

There are many occasions when we ought to be angry. That is, we need to be angry at those who rip off the poor (and anyone else), hurt the helpless, abuse children, misuse their authority, or do anything that is hurtful of others ... or anything that is damaging to God's work and God's world. We need to be angry about pollution, evil, dishonesty, hypocrisy and phoniness. We should be angry at any form of religiosity that keeps people in denial, in bondage, and that is legalistic and controlling. And we need to be angry at any kind of churchianity that keeps people in denial and that doesn't promote healing, wholeness, growth and maturity.

We also ought to be angry at those who champion truth without grace—which is legalism, and at those who promote love without truth—which is little short of sentimental sloppiness. These and a myriad of other evils in the world in which we live we ought to be angry about—and do something about because healthy anger means that we not only feel angry, but that we do something about the circumstances that anger us to bring about change.

Reality is that if we don't get angry at things that are wrong, evil and damaging and do something to bring about change, chances are we don't care that much about things that are right and healing either.

Another way to look at healthy anger is to hate the things that God hates and love the things that he loves. For example: "There are six things the Lord hates, seven that are detestable to him: haughty eyes, a lying tongue, hands that shed innocent blood, a heart that devises wicked schemes, feet that are quick to rush into evil, a false witness who pours out lies and a man who stirs up dissension among brothers."[11]

Think of Florence Nightingale. It would be easy to conjure

up a picture in one's mind of a very gentle, kind, and loving lady. She was all of these, but much more. She was very angry at the way wounded soldiers were being treated. It was her anger that motivated her to do something about the dreadful conditions and poor nursing care the wounded were receiving—or were not receiving.

❏ *Bad anger*

Bad or unhealthy is anger that is misdirected or misappropriated, that is out of proportion to what happened, that is an overreaction to past unresolved events, and/or is for the wrong motive. Much of this anger comes from repressed and unresolved anger from the past that is being acted out in the present. It can come out as hatred, resentment, rage, hostility, abuse, violence, etc. Following are some examples of bad anger:

- When anger is used for selfish reasons by someone to get his or her own way.
- When it is used to lash out and hurt other people.
- When it used to keep people from getting close to you.
- When it is used by boundary-busters who have little or no respect for other people's rights or boundaries. "What part of 'no' don't you under stand?" is a good counter for these people.
- When it is used as a means to control other people. People who use anger in this fashion can be very inhibiting. As long as you can see through their game, however, you can call their bluff by not allowing thei behavior to control you. When they can't control you in this manner, they will either get angrier or quit using it—at least on you.
- When it is repressed and comes out in dirty digs,

snide remarks, negative comments, constantly run
ning late, passive aggressive behavior, ignoring
important appointments, rude remarks, biting sa
castic humor, and so on.

- When a person withdraws when he is angry instead
  of being open and honest with his feelings.
  Withdrawal is a weak way of handling anger and a
  dirty way to fight. It is not Christian in any way,
  shape or form.

- When anger is used to blame somebody else for
  one's own reaction and behavior.

- When it is an overreaction. This is when a present
  situation triggers unresolved anger from the past and
  the reaction is out of proportion to the current incident.

- When anger is used as a defense against fear.
  Instead of admitting and stating that he is feeling
  afraid, this person uses anger to keep from feeling
  his fear. He may even think he is being honest
  because he is sharing his feelings, but if his anger
  is a defense against feeling his fear, he is not being
  honest at all. Actually, a considerable amount of
  anger is a defense against feeling fear. It just feels a
  lot safer to be angry than to be afraid.

In some situations it can be helpful to feel anger if we are
being threatened or abused—depending on the occasion. This
is a self-protective device. If you tease an animal, for example,
and it feels threatened, it will get angry to protect itself.

I ride a mountain bike for exercise and on one occasion
an unfriendly dog came after me attempting to attack me
from behind and grab at my leg. I was not only scared, I was
furious. I swung my bike around (fell off in the process) and
went on the attack. Quickly grabbing a rock, I growled fiercely,
yelled at my attacker, ran towards it and threw the rock with

all my might—all at the same time. What a sight! I missed the dog but it went for its life! I scared it half to death—and hoped that nobody witnessed my roadside episode.

More recently when I was riding my bike in my neighborhood I came across two fairly large dogs going after a mother with a baby in a stroller and a small child walking beside her. The mother and child were terrified. The little girl fell over trying to escape the dogs. I was so thankful that I came on the scene at that moment. Again, I was absolutely furious with these dogs, jumped off my bike and used it to charge at the dogs, yelling at them furiously. Like frightened puppy dogs, with tails between their legs they went for their life. (I also called the city council to report dogs being allowed out on the streets without supervision.)

Sometimes, it is wise to treat bullies the same way— although that can be dangerous, too, if the bully is bigger and stronger than we are. Nevertheless, being in touch with our anger can stop many a person from mistreating and/or walking over us.

Good grief, bad grief

❏ *Good grief*

Good, healthy grief is a normal response to life's losses. It may be the loss of a loved one or a loved object. It is nature's way to relieve the pain and stress of sorrow.

We are created for relationships and cannot live a fulfilling life without them. When we try to, we die a little within every day. We get attached and bonded to people and when we lose someone we love dearly—through death, divorce, separation, rejection or for whatever reason—it can be excruciatingly painful. We experience gut-wrenching, agonizing pain that hurts deeply.

Other losses also cause grief, such as the loss of health, loss of a meaningful job, loss of one's home, income, or other items of importance to us.

Like good anger, grief is meant to be expressed. Tears are nature's way for doing this. They drain away the pain and the hurt from loss. It is damaging to both physical and emotional health to bottle up grief's tears. According to Dr. McMillen, "Not only the emotions of hate and fear are capable of causing a variety of serious and fatal diseases. The emotion of sorrow can also damage the body. Grief can trigger onsets of ulcerative colitis, rheumatoid arthritis, asthma, and many other diseases." That is, if it isn't wept out and resolved.[12]

Medical science has shown that grief's tears have a healing effect as they have a different chemical composition than normal tears. When severe sorrow is experienced, the body produces damaging toxins that tears help to drain away. To rid ourselves of these damaging toxins and release the pain, we need to sob with all our heart for as long as it takes to drain away the pain. In some cases this may happen over a period of days, weeks, or even months, depending on the severity of the loss.

❏ *Bad grief*

Bad grief may look and feel like grief, but it's no more grief than lust is love. It can be a cover-up of anger and expressed as a childish "I'm hurt" crying or be "crocodile tears" that are an attempt to gain sympathy, or get one's own way.

Kids can learn early in life to use crocodile tears. One of my sons hated peas and still does—there are some vegetables that I hated too so I had no argument with his not liking peas. When he was about five or so, his mother wouldn't give him any dessert until he ate his peas. Fat chance. He just sat there moping. His mother got very firm with him so he cried. In frustration she picked up his plate of uneaten peas and stomped off into the kitchen with them. At that moment he looked up at me, grinned sheepishly and said, "It always works!" Kids! He now has one of his own and I couldn't wish it on a nicer person when his kid hates peas or whatever!

He learned to manipulate his mother with tears. As a kid I learned to manipulate my mother by grinning at her when she got mad at me. It always worked too!

Back to hurt feelings. These are because of the pain we feel when we have been slighted, ignored, criticized, or rejected. They are normal feelings when in proportion to what has happened to us. When out of proportion, they are usually hooking into unresolved hurt from the past or triggering our feelings of poor self-worth.

The more hurt that I have unresolved and bottled up from the past, the more I will be supersensitive to life's present hurts and the slightest rebuttal or difference may trigger my tank full of hurt. As a general rule, people who hurt too easily have been hurt somewhere in the past and have never resolved their feelings related to those experiences. Unresolved, these emotions can keep us depressed and sometimes wallowing in self-pity.

Nature's way to resolve grief and genuine feelings of hurt is to cry. However, when tears are from self-pity, or used as a means to avoid feeling and dealing with anger, or as a means of manipulation, they are "crocodile tears" and will neither take away the hurt nor resolve the anger.

Also, when we cry when we are angry, we give up our power. Anger is a power emotion. To deal with it we need to get connected to it, acknowledge it, feel it, and learn to handle and express it creatively. In this way you take your power and learn to stand up for yourself, guard your boundaries, and fight for right.

While in our culture it can still be really tough to get through; nevertheless, men need to be taught that it is okay to cry and women that it is okay and acceptable to feel and show their anger as long as it is in appropriate ways! That is, men need to be given a safe place to get in touch with their grief and learn to sob it out. And women need to be shown that it is not unladylike to feel angry and express it appropriately. It is extremely freeing and healing for both men and women when they learn to do this.

❏ The bottom line

As a general rule grief is the bottom line emotion in all painful experiences. With loss there is often anger but beneath that is grief that needs to be experienced, expressed, and released if healing and recovery are to occur. As Jesus said, "Blessed are those who mourn, for they will be comforted."[13] And as the psalmist wrote, "Weeping may endure for a night, but joy comes in the morning."[14]

Only when we have resolved our anger and sobbed out all our grief do we experience comfort, joy and healing. People who are still bemoaning their losses from years long past have never adequately expressed their grief and anger in meaningful ways ... nor are they likely to recover until they do.

Again, to heal it we need to feel it. To feel it we need to relive it. To relive it we need to bring the memories of past hurtful experiences into the present. And to resolve it we need to express and get rid of all the negative feelings connected to those past painful events.

On one occasion a lady came to me at the close of a seminar session and asked, "Is it really possible to fully get over grief?"

"Yes, it is," I replied and continued, "while we don't forget our losses, when we have resolved our grief related to them ... when we are no longer angry or crying over these losses ... and when we no longer have a need to keep talking about our losses except in a casual way on occasion—then we are freed from and over our grief!"

Good fear, bad fear

Fear is another God-given emotion, a protective survival factor. As with most emotions there is both a healthy and an unhealthy use of this emotion. In other words, there is good fear and bad fear.

❑ *Good fear*

I rightly fear—or should fear—crossing the road against or driving through a red light, traveling or hitchhiking in unsafe places, riding with a driver who has been drinking, associating with toxic people, and so on. Without a good, healthy fear some of us would kill ourselves.

Actually, if more of us were in touch with our good fear, we would save ourselves many difficulties. For example, we ought to be afraid of not maintaining a well-balanced diet, of not getting enough exercise and rest, of drinking too much alcohol, of marrying someone on the basis of romantic feelings or physical attraction alone, of taking unnecessary risks such as driving when we are too sleepy, etc., etc. Good fear keeps us alive, safe, and healthy. Ignore it and we pay the consequences.

❑ *Bad fear*

Bad, negative or unproductive fear often has to do with negative experiences and unresolved hurts from the past. It can cause us to avoid close relationships because of a fear of being hurt again, or to set ourselves up to fail because we fear success, or to avoid certain situations because of a fear of failure, and so on. Bad fear can become terror if caused by a traumatic event in the past.

A person with unresolved fear may live in a constant state of anxiety, be paranoid and feel that everyone is out to get him, or have present events trigger memories from the past and produce the same feelings that the original event caused.

Fear is a common human condition which can range anywhere from the healthy end of the spectrum (good fear) to the unhealthy end (bad fear). It has been said that there are 365 "fear nots" in the Bible—one for every day of the year.

Learning to trust God is one major antidote for fear. For example, David, before he became king of Israel, had good reason to be afraid. King Saul was extremely jealous of David's abilities and popularity and hunted him down with the intention of killing him. David was on the run for some time but said, "In God I trust; I will not be afraid. What can man do to me?"[15]

However, while trusting God for every area of our life is very productive and helpful, it won't eliminate unresolved bad fears from the past. These need to be acknowledged, confronted and dealt with. They can be caused from feelings of insecurity, or by past events where one has been badly hurt, rejected, abused or mistreated. Individual counseling or group therapy is often needed to resolve these fears.

Good guilt, bad guilt

As we have already discussed true and false guilt in an earlier chapter, allow me to recap the difference between good or true guilt and that of bad or false guilt.

❏ *Good guilt*

Good or true guilt is the result of having done something wrong. Its purpose is to motivate us to own up to what we have done, confess it, make restitution wherever possible, and to seek forgiveness for it. When we do this, real guilt is resolved and goes away.

❏ *Bad guilt*

On the other hand, we can confess false guilt forever but it won't go away because it isn't guilt. It just looks and feels like it. It is a feeling of being dirty, unworthy, or never feeling quite good enough. It can be caused by false teaching where people of certain religious groups or sects, for example, are made to feel guilt if they don't conform to the rules and expectations of the particular group to which they belong.

Or it can be a conditioned or learned response as a result of conditional love. But being learned it can be "unlearned" by recognizing it for what it is, and overcome by becoming open to and receiving unconditional love. Sadly, many a parent uses guilt to control their children. If a child conforms to his parent's wishes, he is given love and approval. If not, love and approval are withheld from him and the child is made to feel guilty and bad.

This kind of false guilt is harmful because it is destructive of one's personality, and is a major hindrance for one to feel okay about himself. This kind of person often feels guilty even when he isn't, and is often plagued by self-doubts. It is also a great hindrance to wholesome, fulfilling relationships.

An individual controlled by false guilt or any other unresolved negative emotion is not free to be controlled by love.

False guilt can also be a characteristic of a psychological disorder such as OCD (Obsessive Compulsive Disorder), which can have an emotional as well as a biological component that is best treated by professional help as medication may be needed to offset the chemical imbalance in the brain.

The road less traveled

Truth is the road to recovery and love is the key to healing. The "Truth Road" can be a narrow, winding, uphill path but it is the only way to healing, recovery and love. To be open to receive love, we need to be open and honest with what we truly feel, and empty out and get rid of all of the negative emotions that keep us bound within.

Again, as Peter put it, "Get rid of your feelings of hatred [and all other negative emotions]. Don't just pretend to be good ... Long to grow up into the fullness of your salvation."[16] In the following chapter we will discuss helpful ways to "get rid of" negative emotions and therein find healing for our damaged emotions.

Footnotes:

1. John 1:47, (TLB).
2. Psalm 51:6, (NIV).
3. Psalm 90:12, (NIV).
4. Proverbs 27:5.
5. Peter 2:1-2, (TLB).
6. Philippians 3:13-15, (NIV).
7. Ephesians 4:26-27.
8. John 11:35.
9. Luke 22:44, (NIV).
10. See Matthew 21:12.
11. Proverbs 6:16-19, (NIV).
12. S.I. McMillen, *None of These Diseases* (Westwood, New Jersey: Fleming H. Revell Company, 1963), 103.
13. Matthew 5:4, (NIV).
14. Psalm 30:5.
15. Psalm 56:11, (NIV).
16. 1 Peter 2:1-3, (TLB).

*"I may have been
victimized in the past,
but if I remain
a victim, I am now a
willing volunteer."*

10

The Woman You Gave Me

A NOTE ON A GROCERY store bulletin board, quoted in Barbara Johnson's book, *Stick a Geranium in Your Hat and Be Happy*, reads:

"LOST: DOG with 3 legs, blind in left eye, missing right ear, tail broken, and recently castrated. Answers to the name of Lucky."[1]

"Pain is inevitable," as Tim Hansel puts is, "but misery is optional." Pain is a part of the human journey. But we can choose what we are going to do with it. We can go under because of it, be filled with self-pity and be miserable, or we can accept it as a part of life, use it to help us grow and become better, richer persons—and consider ourselves to be "lucky" (or at least fortunate) too!

Turning pain into gain doesn't happen through wishful thinking or by chance. It takes committed effort on our part, which leads us to our next principle for recovery: Law five: The law of responsibility.

Law five: The law of responsibility

If anyone ever blew it, Adam and Eve did. But did they own up to and accept responsibility for what they did? No way.

God didn't create mankind as puppets on a string. Our first parents, Adam and Eve, were given a free will to choose whether to follow God and adhere to his principles for successful living, or whether they would choose to go their own way. They were warned ahead of the dire circumstances should they choose to reject God's instructions. They were given a simple test. In the Garden of Eden God told them that they could eat the fruit of every tree except from the tree of the "Knowledge of Good and Evil."

Sadly, Adam and Eve chose to eat the forbidden fruit.

Enter God: "What have you done Adam? Have you eaten from the tree of the knowledge of good and evil?"

"The woman YOU gave me, God, made me do it," Adam said defending himself. "It's all her fault. Besides, it's really your fault because you gave me this woman."

Then the woman blamed the serpent. "The serpent made me do it," the woman declared. And ever since, people have been avoiding personal responsibility and projecting blame onto God, the devil, the government, or anybody else they can find.

However, foundational for healing and recovery is facing reality and accepting responsibility for both our healing and recovery—and, as already stated, avoiding the blame game at all cost. Remember, "If we play the blame game, we will B-LAME!"

M. Scott Peck said, "Emotional heath is facing reality at any cost. Emotional illness is avoiding reality at any cost." It is imperative, therefore, that we admit and accept responsibility for all our sins, mistakes, and problems. This includes not only external acts of sin, but having mixed motives and unresolved, supercharged repressed negative emotions from past hurtful experiences. All of these need to be brought into the light,[2] to be resolved.

Resolving negative emotions drains away grief, resentment, and bitterness, and opens the door for physical, emotional, and spiritual healing, as well as freeing us to forgive all who have hurt us. This is also essential for overcoming addictive and negative behavior patterns—which are often used to medicate and avoid facing our painful unresolved emotions.

Again, it isn't sufficient to merely talk about our problems or about our feelings. If that's all we ever do, we can get stuck in no-man's-land and stay there forever in a pity party. We need to connect to our feelings and express them in healthy ways to get them out of our system—to get rid of them, and put them behind us.

Expressing negative emotions creatively releases us from the past so we can move towards developing our total human and spiritual potential—and become the person God envisioned us to be. Failing to do so can inhibit our progress, stop our growth, kill our joy, and keep life *wonder-empty* rather than *wonder-full*. It can also cause us to become physically ill, take years off our life, and damage or destroy our relationships.

Furthermore, unless we express our negative emotions in healthy ways, we will in one way or another express them in unhealthy ways. When triggered, they can cause us to explode and lash out and hurt others, or implode and turn our painful emotions inward and hurt ourselves. Doing the latter can cause depression, anxiety, stress, or any of a number of physical ailments, and/or adversely affect our relationships with others and with God. This is because unresolved negative emotions cause a barrier to come between us and God and between us and others.

When I bury my negative emotions, I bury my positive emotions with them. To put it another way, the walls I put around my heart to block out my negative emotions also surround my positive emotions and block them out too. Only as I can feel with all my heart, am I able to love with all my heart. And only as I can fully feel my grief and anger, can I fully feel my love and joy. They go hand in hand.

We simply cannot afford not to obey the biblical injunction to get rid of our feelings of hatred and all other negative emotions, The Bible also says, "Since we have such a huge crowd of men of faith watching us from the grandstands [those men of faith watching us from heaven] let us strip off anything that slows us down or holds us back, and especially those sins that wrap themselves so tightly around our feet and trip us up; and let us run with patience the particular race that God has set before us."[3] It's not only external acts of sins that trip us up and hold us back, but also unresolved sins such as hurt, anger, grief, bitterness, fears, and so on.

David wrote, "Surely you [God] desire truth in the inner parts; you teach me wisdom in the inmost place."[4] And again, "Search me, O God, and know my heart; test me and know my anxious thoughts. See if there is any offensive way in me, and lead me in the way everlasting."[5]

Unresolved supercharged negative emotions are hidden secrets of the heart, or "sins of the spirit" that contaminate every part of our life and well-being. They are very damaging to human personality and relationships. This is why God wants us to be aware of them, be truthful about them, and resolve and be rid of them. The rest of this chapter will show how this can be achieved.

Ten steps for resolving negative emotions

❑ *Step one, a reminder: don't blame others for your difficulties*

I can blame my parents for the problems I have, or my spouse, my employer, lover, friend, or even God, but unless

I quit blaming others and accept full responsibility for the problems and feelings I have and the actions I have taken, I will never overcome my problems nor be free from their effects on me.

True, I may not have been responsible for hurtful things that happened to me in the past, especially as a child, but as an adult I am totally responsible for resolving my issues and for what I become. Nobody else is going to do it for me. In fact, as an adult, unless I am severely handicapped, I am totally responsible for every area of my life. As somebody else has suggested, "I may have been victimized in the past, but if I remain a victim I am now a willing volunteer."

When I look back, it is to understand what is, not to dwell on what was, or to place the blame for my problems on somebody else. If I am still angry at my parents, I need to realize that they, too, were the products of their background who, in turn, were the products of their background, and so on for generations past.

Only as I face and resolve my issues, can I help break the chain from the past and not pass on to my children the problems I "inherited" (learned) from my parents. The fact is we raise not the children we want, but basically the children that we the parents are.

If there is one thing I need to do to overcome my past, it is to program into my belief system that I am responsible for my life—for what I do about my past and for what I become.

❏ *Step two: realize that whatever bothers me is my problem*

What somebody else did to me may or may not be a problem. Whatever they did is his or her issue and responsibility. How I respond and react is always my responsibility. If I perceive what he or she did as being negative and feel hurt and angry as a result, it is important to remember that those are my feelings—and my feelings are always my responsibility. Until

I resolve these feelings, they are my problem. Whether my feelings are justified or not is not the issue. The issue is what my reaction was to what happened, how I felt about it, and what I did or didn't do about it.

When bad things happen to me, if I act appropriately—that is, in proportion to what happened—my response is still my responsibility to deal with. But when I overreact—that is, out of proportion to what happened—to the degree that I do is totally my problem and my responsibility to resolve.

I know this can be difficult to accept, and I am not saying that we shouldn't react. Not at all. But keep in mind that we always react and/or overreact on the basis of who we are—not on the basis of what happened to us. We overreact when what happens in the present gets hooked into and triggers unresolved hurt, anger, and so on from the past. Also, we often react to present situations on the basis of how we learned to react to the same or similar experiences in the past.

Only as I admit that my upset is my problem and my responsibility can I resolve and overcome it.

❏ *Step three: acknowledge and take ownership of my feelings*

We gain a deep sense of freedom when we acknowledge the fact that, at best, our feelings are triggered from outside influences but are not caused by them. As adults, we need to realize that people don't hurt us or make us feel angry or anything else without our permission. Thus, to resolve our feelings, we need to admit what our feelings are and take ownership of them. (Actually, if we had a perfect self-concept—which very few, if any, do—it would take a lot to get our feelings hurt over what somebody does to us.)

❏ *Step four: confess nobody's sins but our own*

When resolving our feelings, it is necessary to mention

briefly who did what to us, but if we keep condemning the other person and talking about what they did (as hurtful as it may have been), it won't help because confessing their "sins" won't resolve ours. In fact, it will increase ours if we remain bitter and resentful. Whatever it was that happened to us, we need to say how that made us feel and concentrate on expressing and resolving our feelings, and not dwell on what the other person did.

My suggestion when dealing with people, either in one-on-one counseling or in a growth or recovery group, is to ask participants to keep the history of what happened as brief as possible and get into the feelings behind what happened. Dwelling on the history (his-story) of what happened keeps us stuck. Only as we acknowledge what our feelings are and get them out of our system, are we freed from them.

☐ *Step five: learn to accept other's feelings without being judgmental, giving advice, or trying to fix them*

Whenever I ask people how to grow in love, almost one-hundred percent say by loving others. The problem with this is that we cannot give what we haven't got. To put it another way, only to the degree that we have learned to love and accept ourselves in a healthy way are we able to love and accept others in a healthy way. The way we learn to love and accept ourselves is the same way we learn to love God. We love him because he first loved us.[6] We, too, need somebody to first accept and love us.

The way to do this is by allowing one or two trusted friends (or a counselor if necessary) see the real us—warts and all—and by their accepting and loving us just as we are. Through their love and acceptance of us, little by little we learn to love and accept ourselves. Furthermore, we can only be loved and accepted to the degree that we are known. That is, to be fully loved we need to be fully known.

143

When others take the risk, open up and share their sins, failures, and feelings with us, and we preach at them, criticize or put them down, give them advice or try to fix them, they won't feel accepted or loved and their problems will be reinforced. If they are at all sensitive, it will make them feel worse.

Furthermore, we cannot change anybody else but ourselves. We may wish we could, but we can't. And as long as we try to change or fix anybody else, we not only make them angrier, but we also avoid facing our own problems. Our responsibility is to change ourselves—not anybody else. As the Bible advises, "Rid yourself [not somebody else] of all malice."[7]

Generally speaking, as we change, it is interesting to see how others around us tend to change! In fact, they are almost forced to change one way or another—not always for the best, however, as many people do not want us to change or to stop playing their destructive games. Some will show intense resistance. To become real and grow can thus put our relationships at risk. However, not to become real and grow also puts our relationships at risk as it is impossible to have close, intimate relationships with people who are not real, nor open and honest with their true feelings.

Unfortunately, too many would-be-fixers are cursed with the affliction to give advice. Advice giving, especially where it's neither wanted nor asked for, implies that the advice-giver knows more than the other person knows about his problems. It can be a one-upmanship game. Furthermore, as long as we advise others and tell them what they should do, we keep them over-dependent on us; that is, if they listen to us, which mostly they don't. If they do listen to us and heed our words, it stops their accepting responsibility for making their own decisions and growing up.

It is far better to help others see their options so they can decide for themselves what is the best and right for them to do. Remember, too, that they are better off making their own decisions even if they are wrong, than forever being over-dependent on others to tell them what they need to do and making their decisions for them.

If giving advice worked and if we could fix others, there wouldn't be any problems left in the world. But advice giving doesn't work and the only person we can ever fix is our self. What we and others need when sharing our feelings and problems is a listening and a loving, accepting heart—not advice giving or fixing.

❏ Step six: stay focused

"Just as chronic absenteeism can be an unconscious avoidance of some painful area, there is a tendency for people who do not want to face some personal defect to change the subject if the discussion begins to get painful. Usually this is completely unconscious, and is often rationalized very skillfully."[8]

We are probably all guilty of having done this as it is so much easier and considerably more comfortable to avoid the subject than to face it. However, to resolve painful feelings it is essential to stay focused on the issue at hand, and not change the subject.

❏ Step seven: avoid being defensive

Recently a man whom I didn't trust took me aside to tell me that he felt hurt by me. He wanted to be a friend but felt that I was shutting him out.

From the day I met this man, I didn't trust him. His feelings were right. I was shutting him out of my personal space. I had no intention of letting him in or of being a close friend. So when he told me how he felt, I simply answered, "I accept your feelings. Thank you for sharing them with me." That's all I had to say. I shook his hand and went my way.

I felt no need to be defensive nor did I feel a need to explain my position to this man. I learned soon afterwards that he was angry at me because I wouldn't apologize to him. I wasn't sorry so I didn't pretend I was.

Interestingly enough, a few weeks later this man was asked to leave the particular group we were in. He had apparently been trying to manipulate certain women in the group for ulterior motives. I'm glad that I remained true to my gut feelings, which proved to be on target.

When attacked or criticized, if I am not guilty, why does it bother me? If I have done something wrong, or even if I haven't but feel hurt, angry, or threatened, getting defensive avoids facing the issue at hand and blocks resolution.

❑ *Step eight: use "I" messages, not "you" messages*

Counselors have been telling us the following for quite a while now, but it can still be very difficult and challenging to do. That is, when sharing your feelings directly with the person whom you feel has offended or hurt you, be sure to use "I" messages. Doing this accepts responsibility for what you are feeling. Using "you" messages blames the other person for your reactions. Saying, "You make me mad," can also put the other person on the defensive and he may become angry back at you!

It is considerably more constructive to express feelings by saying something like, "I have a problem and need to talk to you about it. I feel what you did was not called for and I feel hurt and/or angry about this. I know my anger is my problem, but I'd like to discuss this matter with you."

❑ *Step nine: speak the truth in love*

Speaking the truth for the wrong reason is rarely helpful and can be very hurtful. I may speak the truth to somebody whom I felt has hurt me, but if I don't do so in a spirit of love,[9] I may do more to hurt, rather than help, that person and our relationship. I may pretend to act in a loving manner, but if I do it with mixed motives for self-centered reasons, it is neither truthful nor loving.

Furthermore, without love, truth is going to be kept hidden or denied. "Grace and truth came by Jesus Christ."[10] Grace, which is unconditional love and unmerited favor, always needs to precede truth. For example, if you feel that I have hurt or offended you, but don't feel that I will offer you grace (loving acceptance), you will not feel safe to share your true feelings with me—and understandably so. And the rift between us may never be resolved.

If I have a need to confess my sins and faults to someone whom I feel won't offer me grace, then I am not going to open up to that person. We only grow in a loving and accepting atmosphere. We were damaged in unloving, non-accepting, damaging relationships and find healing only in loving and accepting relationships.

When we have a need to confront anybody, we need to be certain that we are speaking the truth in love. This doesn't mean that we don't show anger. Not at all. But when we express anger, we need to do so in a loving way with the purpose of reconciliation and for promoting the other person's growth as well as my own. While we don't hide our feelings, we don't have to "yell and scream" to express anger. It can be expressed in a firm, yet loving way.

❏ *Step ten: share feelings not thoughts or opinions*

As already noted, talking about our problems and sharing only our thoughts about them doesn't resolve either the problem nor heal our feelings. Feelings need to be felt and then expressed. Remember, what we don't talk out or express creatively we will inevitably act out destructively in one way or another.

As mentioned in the previous chapter, there are at least four major areas of negative emotions that need resolution. They are: anger, grief, fear, and guilt—emotions that need to be felt and experienced in the present and expressed in creative ways. For example:

Anger needs to be verbalized. Directed physical activity as well as verbalization can also help release tension caused by anger. By directed I mean, if you have an overwhelming urge to hit, never, never hit people. If needs be, punch a punching bag, chop a pile of wood, or go for a vigorous run or walk.

Grief needs to be sobbed out.

Fear, probably the most challenging emotion to resolve, also needs to be felt and verbalized. If it is terror, it may need to be screamed out. After the fear and/or terror is expressed, then feelings need to be reconditioned by facing the fear and doing the thing we are afraid to do—just one "baby step" at a time—and never in too big a hurry.

And *guilt* (genuine guilt, that is, and not false guilt) needs to be confessed and, wherever possible, restitution made.

Six ways to resolve negative emotions creatively

❏ *First, pray*

Tell God about your problem and express your feelings to him. Tell him exactly how you feel and ask him to give you the courage to recognize and accept all your feelings and, where necessary, to confront and talk to the person who hurt you. Also, ask God to help you to be as Christ to this person and to speak the truth in love to him, to help you to forgive him, and wherever possible to help you heal the impaired relationship.

❏ *Second, share your feelings with the person who hurt or angered you*

148

Wherever possible, usually the most productive way to handle and resolve anger and hurt is, as early as possible, to go directly to the person you feel angry towards and share your feelings with him or her, not forgetting to use "I" messages. As Jesus said, "If you are standing before the altar in the Temple, offering a sacrifice to God, and suddenly remember that a friend has something against you, leave your sacrifice there beside the altar and go and apologize and be reconciled to him and then come and offer your sacrifice to God."[11] The same principle applies if we have something against another person.

❑ *Third, express feelings to an understanding friend,*
   counselor, or support/recovery group

Sometimes it may do more harm than good to share directly with the person who hurt you, especially if he/she is unloving and non-accepting.

Some people claim that the only one we need to confess to is to God and that will bring healing. While we need to confess to God, we also need to confess to at least one other trusting person. It is not without good reason that the Bible says, "Therefore confess your sins to each other and pray for each other so that you may be healed."[12]

While we can do some recovery work alone, we also need to do some, if not most of it, with at least one other loving, accepting, non-judgmental person, or where necessary (depending on the degree of the hurt) with a qualified counselor and, in time, with a qualified support group.

❑ *Fourth, another option is to write out your feelings*

Writing out feelings is another very effective way to express feelings and get them off your chest and out of your system. This is what David did in the Psalms, many of which are an expression of his emotions. David was a man very much in tune with and honest about his feelings. I'm sure this is why he was known as a man after God's own heart.[13] It certainly wasn't because of his behavior—especially regarding his adultery with Bathsheba, getting her pregnant—then having her husband killed so he could marry her in a vain attempt to cover what he had done. But God knew and confronted David through the prophet, Nathan. Then David admitted what he had done and was honest with his feelings.

He not only confessed to Nathan, but also wrote out his feelings. When he felt guilty, he wrote out those feelings. When he was happy, he wrote about those feelings. When he was thankful, he expressed those feelings in writing. When he was sad he wrote out those feelings. And when he was hurt and angered by false accusers and by those who were jealous of him and hated him, he also expressed those feelings in writing.[14]

We can do the same with our feelings. Write to the person who hurt you and empty out all the hurt and angry feelings you have towards him or her. Read the letter out loud to God, to yourself and perhaps to a trusted friend or counselor, then tear it up and throw it away; and do that again and again until all the hurt and anger are gone. Should you feel a need to mail the letter to the person involved, may I again suggest that you never ever send the first draft. Remember, the biblical principal to use when sharing your hurt or angry feelings (either written or spoken) is to "speak the truth in love."[15] The letter you mail needs to be written in a loving way and not used as a means of dumping on another person or taking out your unresolved issues on them.

Keep in mind, though, that what is in writing can be used against you by a vitriolic person, so be very cautions about doing this. If you still feel a need to do this, it would be wise to have your counselor or perhaps even your lawyer, edit your letter before it is mailed.

❏ *Fifth, use some self-help therapy*

While most healing comes as we resolve our hurts in healing relationships (such as with a qualified counselor), some recovery work can be done alone. Barbara Johnson suggests a helpful way to accelerate healing.

She spoke about a Christian lady who worked as a salesperson but had a terrible time at work. She had recently lost a child but couldn't stop crying when she was trying to wait on a customer. Here's the plan Barbara suggested:

"Get some sad music tapes, the saddest you can find. Make sure everyone is out of the house, then go to the bedroom, unplug the phone, turn on the sad music, flop on the bed and just sob. Set a timer for thirty minutes and, during that time, cry and pound the pillow. Let out your feelings—ventilate. If you're angry at God, that's OK. He won't say, 'Off to hell with you.' He still loves you. But get those deep hurts out through the avenue of tears. Do that every day for thirty days and every day set your timer for one minute less. By the time thirty days have passed, you will have dumped a lot of your cup of grief."[16]

As Jesus said, "Blessed are they who mourn, for they shall be comforted."[17] David wrote, "Happy are those who are strong in the Lord, who want above all else to follow your steps. When they walk through the Valley of Weeping it will become a place of springs where pools of blessing and refreshment collect after rains! They will grow constantly in strength."[18]

This is a creative way to help get anger out too. Instead of crying, express the anger verbally while thumping the pillow. Doing this won't hurt you and it won't hurt the pillow. It's much wiser to hit a pillow than hitting your kids. Or go for a drive in your car, wind up the windows, turn up the radio, and pretend the person you are mad at is sitting beside you and share your feelings with him or her.

This can be helpful, too, if the person you are angry at is dead or gone from your life. Imagine he or she is there with you and say everything you need to say as if he/she were. The important thing is to get all your negative feelings off your chest and out of your system. Personally speaking, I went to my father's graveside to have a little "chat" with him, which proved to be another helpful step in my healing and recovery. By the way, I did this alone! I took a pad and pen with me and at the conclusion of our three-hour visit, I "asked" my dad, "If you were still living today, what would you like to say to me?" The answer that came to me (in my head) was this: "Don't let your pain control you, and don't allow your past to determine your future." That's great advice for anyone.

❑ *Sixth, use role-play*

Another effective way for accelerating the healing process is similar to Barbara Johnson's method. It can be through role-play which some counselors call psychodrama.

First, though, a word of caution: role-play where individuals have strong emotions needs to be directed by a well-trained qualified counselor and/or group leader. It should not be done by untrained individuals.

Role-play can be done one-on-one with a counselor who "sits in" for the person who has hurt and even terrified you. You imagine the counselor is that person and express your feelings to him/her as if they were the real person. Some counselors have you sit opposite an empty chair and imagine the person who has hurt you is sitting in that chair. This may need to be done a number of times but can be very effective too.

Even more effective is what I like to call spiritual-drama or simply prayer-counseling. I call it this because in the workshops I have directed in the past, we incorporated prayer and had people role-play God and Jesus as well as role-playing other people. I actually got this idea from a secular workshop I was in. One lady (who had no idea that I was a Christian) asked me if I would role-play God for her. I felt momentarily stunned, but after the initial shock, I agreed to do so. She had me sit in a chair in the center of the group and, not having any idea what she was going to do or say, I kept praying under my breath, "Help, God, help!"

This lady then knelt in front of me and began to confess her sins (of a very personal nature) and asked me (though in her heart she was asking God, not me) for forgiveness. Immediately the words of Jesus came to mind when the woman caught in adultery was brought to him, so I said to this lady, "Your sins are forgiven." I found this to be a very humbling, enlightening, and helpful experience.

Often people feel not only guilty before God, but are also angry at him. Role-playing for some can be an extremely effective method to get that anger out. I recall vividly the experience of one man in one of our groups whose wife had died of cancer several years before. Before she died, both he and she were convinced that God was going to heal her. But God didn't. She died when their children were still small. I will never forget the day Jonathon (not his real name) asked a group member, with whom he felt safe, if he would role-play God for him, to which the man agreed. Jonathon poured out several years of bottled-up emotions of intense grief and anger to God. I don't think there were any dry eyes in the room that day—including mine—as Jonathon sobbed out intense grief and sorrow, and was totally honest with God with his angry feelings towards him.

Because Jonathon was so real and courageously honest, we felt we were standing on holy ground. A sense of God's presence filled the room. It was not only a deeply emotional experience but an intense spiritual experience. This experience proved to be a marvelous beginning of Jonathon's healing. It helped him overcome his fear of loving and freed him to love again. Soon after, he found a new love. How true is God's word that says, "The LORD is near to all who call on him, to all who call on him in truth."[19]

As already noted, when we bottle up our feelings of grief and other negative emtions, we also bottle up and block our feelings of love. And while it may sound somewhat crude, when we stuff (repress and deny) our feelings, it gives us "emotional constipation" that poisons our whole system—physically, emotionally, spiritually, and relationally.

And when we are angry at God, he knows it anyhow so the best thing to do is to confess and express it to him. He doesn't get upset when we are angry at him any more than I got upset when my kids were angry at me. What I wanted them to do was give me their anger; that is, express it to me verbally without yelling at me, so we could resolve the issue at hand and be close again. God wants us to do the same with him. It's insecure parents who get shook up when their kids get mad at them. I never allowed my kids to hit me, but I always encouraged them to tell me how they felt. I may not have agreed with them, but I hope I always accepted their feelings and that, even as adults, they will always feel safe to share their feelings with me.

Getting back to role-play. In such a group a participant may be angry at or feel hurt by several members of his family so he has different group members represent the various family members, and expresses to them everything he or she needs to get off his or her chest.

Someone else may be angry at a boss and have somebody represent the boss. Or they may be angry at an abuser and have someone substitute for that person. Someone else may have been rejected, divorced, or abandoned and have someone represent the person who hurt them. The list could go on and on. Genuine role-playing by whatever name we call it is another effective way to "get rid of feelings of hatred, etc."

We need to go over each issue until we are no longer crying, afraid, guilty, or angry. When we connect to our pain, bring it to the light,[20] and express it creatively until it dissipates and goes away (which is not going to happen overnight), we will finally be set free—free to forgive, free to love, and free to move on with our lives according to God's plan for us.

We simply cannot improve on God's plan for healthy and dynamic living—the principles for which are given in God's Word, the Bible. We just need to apply them in our daily life. Whatever method we use is not important. What is necessary is that we find the way that works best for us so that we resolve all our hurt, grief, guilt, fear, anger, and all bottled up negative emotions.

And then learn to resolve hurt feelings as close as possible to the hurtful event. As the Bible teaches, "Don't let the sun go down on your anger" or any other painful feelings.[21] And be sure to get rid of your feelings of hatred[22] and all other negative emotions.

Again, we may not have been responsible for what happened to us in the past, but as adults (and teens who have reached the age of responsibility), we are totally responsible for what we do about resolving our past, for getting rid of all our hurt and resentful feelings, for forgiving all who have hurt us, and for putting the past behind us so we can truly say with Paul, "But one thing I do: Forgetting what is behind and straining toward what is ahead, I press on toward the goal to win the prize for which God has called me heavenward in Christ Jesus."[23]

Footnotes

1. Barbara Johnson, *Stick a Geranium in Your Hat and Be Happy* (Dallas, Texas: Word Incorporated, 1990), 1.
2. See 1 John 1:7.
3. Hebrews 12:1, (TLB).
4. Psalm 51:6, (NIV).
5. Psalm 139:23-24, (NIV).
6. 1 John 4:19.
7. 1 Peter 2:1, (NIV).
8. Cecil G. Osborne, *New Dimensions in Spiritual Growth* (Millbrae, California: Yokefellows, Inc.), 4.
9. Ephesians 4:15.
10. John 1:17.
11 Matthew 5:23-24, (TLB).
12. James 5:16, (NIV).
13. Acts 13:22.
14. See Psalm 109.
15. Ephesians 4:15.
16. Barbara Johnson, *Stick a Geranium in Your Hat and Be Happy*, 29-30.
17. Matthew 5:4.
18. Psalm 84:5-7, (TLB).
19. Psalm 145:18, (NIV).
20. 1 John 1:7.
21. Ephesians 4:26.
22. 1 Peter 2:1-2.
23. Philippians 3:13-14, (NIV).

"Blessed is the one ... Whose
delight is in the law of the LORD,
and on his law he meditates day and
night. He is like a tree planted by streams
of water, which yields its fruit in season
and whose leaf does not wither.
Whatever he does prospers."

11

Come Apart Before You Come Apart

JOAN BORYSENKO, author, lecturer, and co-founder of the Mind/Body Clinic, New England Deaconess Hospital, Harvard Medical School, had been troubled by migraines all her life. By the time she was twenty-four, as a medical student, she was already a physical wreck. Besides having migraines, she suffered from crippling stomach pains, vomiting, severe bronchitis, high blood pressure, and fainting spells.

When Dr. Borysenko first heard how meditation could help in the healing process, she said, "My first thought was that meditation was for ascetics who lived in caves. I was a hard-headed scientist, literally killing myself to master the ways of the medical establishment.

"Nevertheless," she said, "I gave it a try—largely out of desperation—practicing each day."[1]

A few weeks later while she was sitting at her electronic microscope she felt the symptoms of a migraine attack coming on so she retreated to her office, pulled the shades and shut the door. She breathed deeply to help her relax and began to meditate. In time the pain subsided. After the meditation was over, she had a feeling of "having been washed clean, like the earth after a heavy rain."[2] Dr. Borysenko had "discovered" for herself, the sixth commandment of healing and growth: the law of meditation and relaxation.

While some people are negative towards meditation, it is at least as old as the Bible. It is actually amazing how long it has taken modern medicine to catch up with what the Bible taught three thousand years ago. In the Psalms David wrote: "Blessed is the man ... whose delight is in the law of the LORD, and on his law he meditates day and night. He is like a tree planted by streams of water, which yields its fruit in season and whose leaf does not wither. Whatever he does prospers."[3]

Law six: The law of relaxation and meditation

Meditation may be used by New Age adherents but it was not discovered by them, and just because these folk practice it, is no reason to discard or avoid it. Meditation is a form of relaxation that mentally removes one's thoughts for brief periods of time from the pressures, stress, anxiety, and problems of the moment. Through meditation one can separate himself in his mind from his surroundings and circumstances and transport himself to a quiet restful place, clear his mind of all troubling thoughts, be still, and fill his mind with positive thoughts, Scriptures such as the twenty-third Psalm, and visualize in his mind scenes of natural beauty and pictures of well-being.

Learning to relax is essential for all healing and wellness —physical, emotional, and spiritual. As already pointed out, this knowledge is nothing new. Three thousand years ago

King Solomon wrote in the Bible how one's attitude affected one's health. "A heart at peace gives life to the body, but envy rots the bones,"[4] he wrote. Another translation put it this way, "A relaxed attitude lengthens a man's life; jealousy rots it away."

Even Jesus, in the midst of a hectic schedule, walked away from all the people who were in need of his help, and said to his disciples, "Come apart to a quiet place and rest a while."[5] Or as another put it, "Come apart and rest a while before you come apart!" Taking time to "come apart" is essential but even when we can't do so physically, we can always do so in our mind. The effect can be almost as effective.

And God, through King David, said, "Be still, and know that I am God"[6]—a meditative practice that can be very relaxing and can be very healing.

To be still, breathe deeply, relax and meditate upon God and/or a peaceful setting when you are filled with anxiety or bogged down with an overload of responsibilities can be very difficult to do. Workaholics have a difficult time sitting still long enough to meditate. Others have a hard time disciplining their minds to switch off the things that are disturbing them. Given time, with regular practice, these hindrances can be overcome. A daily quiet time plus a few moments of meditation at various times throughout the day can work wonders.

Label me and you negate me

Unfortunately there are some Christians who are afraid of meditation for fear they might open their mind to some unwanted idea or evil force. Or they fear that meditation is dangerous because it is practiced by those in the New Age movement or other questionable groups.

In the past if church people didn't like what someone from another church group was proposing, or if they didn't agree precisely with their particular brand of theology, whether or not they understood what the other group was saying, and whether or not they were right or wrong, if they were afraid of them and what they were standing for, they branded them with a label. The really "bad" ones were labeled heretics, some of whom were burned at the stake in years gone by. In more recent times others have been branded in negative terms such as being liberal, neo-orthodox, contemporary, ultra conservative, a progressive dispensationalist, New Age, etc., etc. Others have been accused of being of the devil. The way these terms were used implied that the one being labeled was dangerous to follow.

To label someone is to negate them. Unfortunately this often negates something that is both legitimate and helpful. We need to be certain not to condemn another's point of view until we at least know and understand it.

In student days I was attending a particular college and recall how the founder of this institution warned students who were going to Chicago in the summer not to attend Moody Memorial Church because the then pastor, Alan Redpath from England, was a silver-tongued liberal orator and, as such, would easily lead us astray. I decided to hear this so-called silver-tongued orator for myself, and after transferring to a college in Chicago, attended his church for some time. I actually found this man to be far from what was considered a liberal. Such gossip can be very destructive of another person and his work.

Interesting, too, how on another occasion, the speaker who accused Alan Redpath of being a liberal silver-tongued orator, said that while many of us would never think of stealing a man's transportation, we wouldn't hesitate to steal his reputation. He was right. He certainly stole Alan Redpath's reputation in the minds of many.

Today there is considerable criticism by many Christians

against psychological counseling claiming that such relieves individuals of personal responsibility. Certainly there is bad counseling just as there is bad theology, bad teaching, and so on. But because one apple in a basket is bad doesn't mean or imply that all the apples are bad. In fact, just the opposite is true because good counseling teaches individuals to be personally honest and avoid denial at all cost, to face reality, to confess their sins and faults, and to take responsibility for their actions and their recovery.

One thing is certain, when accusations are false they can be malicious slander and gossip. Something that, because of its destructive nature, is forbidden by God.[7]

To accuse someone of being liberal, narrow-minded, New Age or anything else for no other reason than the fact that we disagree with (or are afraid of) their teaching without honestly evaluating it, may be closer to being "heretical" than what the critics claim the accused one is teaching.

God or the god within?

This is not to say or imply that we never question what others are teaching. Not so. Certainly we need to be able to discern the difference between what is right and what is wrong, what is dangerous and what is wholesome, what is truth and what is not—and beware of false prophets who come to us in sheep's clothes. To be thus discerning we need to be grounded in the Word of God and know what the Bible teaches.

The central premise of false beliefs and practices is in many ways like New Age thinking in that it is not about God within, but about "the god within" which, in a sense, is equating yourself with God.

"The god within" premise is dangerously close to what Satan did when he became the devil. Isaiah wrote about Lucifer, better known as Satan, the devil, and asked, "How you have fallen from heaven, O morning star, son of the dawn?"[8]

Isaiah then answered his question: "You said in your heart, 'I will ascend to heaven; I will raise my throne above the stars of God; I will sit enthroned on the mount of assembly, on the utmost heights of the sacred mountain. I will ascend above the tops of the clouds; I will make myself like the Most High.' But you are brought down to the grave, to the depths of the pit.[9]

Attempting to put himself above God was Satan's downfall. Pride was his core problem. Pride also caused the first man and woman to fall. Pride is also at the core of New Age thinking, and at the very foundation of those who put their own reasoning above that of God's Word. In other words they play the role of God in matters of morals and practice, and in so doing they put themselves above God—a dangerous path to follow and ultimately self-destructive.

Not everything bad teachers teach is bad

However, as already stated, not everything bad teachers teach is bad nor wrong any more than to say that everything that the Pharisees said or did was wrong. And just because many other groups practice meditation doesn't make meditation wrong or harmful. In fact, every false cult, every false religion, and every false philosophy has an element of truth which makes their teaching both believable and dangerous.

Many of these groups have taken helpful practices from various sources (including from the Bible) and have incorporated them into their own belief system. Meditation happens to be one of these. True, some meditation can be dangerous if one meditates on strange mystical or superstitious thoughts. However in these instances it's the content of the meditation that is dangerous, not the practice of meditation. When we dwell on temptation and keep thinking about whatever it is we are tempted to do, that too is a form of bad meditation.

Webster defines meditation as follows: "to plan or intend; to think deeply." That's something we all need to practice regularly—especially when it comes to thinking deeply on the principles for healthy living found in God's word—and applying them to our daily life.

God's promise of success

Meditation has been around a long time, long before the New Age movement was thought of—like several thousand years before. It comes directly from the pages of the Bible. For instance, God told the ancient Israelites that if they wanted to be successful they would need to meditate on God's Word "day and night" and of course, "obey it."

"Be strong and very courageous," God said. "Be careful to obey all the law my servant Moses gave you; do not turn from it to the right or to the left, that you may be successful wherever you go. Do not let this Book of the Law depart from your mouth; meditate on it day and night, so that you may be careful to do everything written in it. Then you will be prosperous and successful. Have I not commanded you? Be strong and courageous. Do not be terrified; do not be discouraged, for the Lord your God will be with you wherever you go."[10]

David, the psalmist, said a similar thing: "Blessed is the man who ... meditates day and night on God's law."[11] That was written three thousand years ago!

What the mind thinks about comes about

Positive or creative meditation is effective because it relaxes the body and clears the mind of the tensions and pressures of the day to do two things. First, it can bring to mind a truth we need to know, an issue we need to resolve, or an idea we are meant to develop or share with another.

Second, meditation programs helpful thoughts (or negative thoughts if these are what one chooses) into one's deeper memory or unconscious mind. Once there, they strongly affect one's thinking, feelings, and actions. This is why David said, "I have hidden your word in my heart so I won't sin against you."[12]

It is evident that what the mind thinks about comes about, or as another has said, "What the mind dwells on the body acts on." Consider, for example, how temptation works. It starts in the mind as a thought and desire. As we dwell on the thought, the feelings of desire increase which, in turn, feeds our thoughts. And the more we think about it, the stronger we feel about it, and the stronger we feel about it, the more we begin to visualize and justify in our minds what we want to do. If we continue to dwell on the temptation; that is, meditate on it, pretty soon we'll find we are acting it out.

I remember hearing about the man who took second place in the international piano contest where either Richard Clayderman or Van Clyburn took first place. Obviously, he was a very accomplished pianist. Until a few months prior to the contest this man hadn't played a piano in several years as he had been a prisoner of war in Vietnam. After gaining second place, he was asked how was it that he did so well when he hadn't practiced for several years. He went on to explain how, when he was in prison, he pictured in his mind a piano keyboard and practiced diligently on it every day—all in his mind. Such is the power of the human mind. Diligent meditation can have the same kind of effect.

Not what, but how, makes the difference

Meditation can work for good or for bad, depending on how it is used. Meditate on negative thoughts and you will act negatively. Meditate on positive thoughts and you will act positively. Meditation that is healing is that which focuses on a positive and helpful thought such as a comforting Psalm, "The Lord is my shepherd, I shall lack nothing. He makes me lie down in green pastures, he leads me beside quiet waters, he restores my soul."[13] And again, "In God I trust; I will not be afraid. What can man do to me?"[14]

If we constantly meditate on how sick we are and dwell on that thought, we will reinforce our sickness. If, however, we constantly think about getting well and picture being healthy in our mind, that will help promote and speed our healing. As we have already said the writer of the Proverbs said, "A tranquil mind gives life to the body, but envy rots the bones."[15]

How to meditate creatively

First, set a daily quiet time, preferably first thing in the day where you can come apart from the pressures of life to be alone for twenty to thirty minutes with your thoughts and with God. Make this time a habit. This will help set the tone and the "rudder" for your day.

Second, choose a quiet place where you can be alone without interruptions. Switch the telephone off or unplug it. Get up before the rest of the family if necessary. Keep the radio and TV off. Guard this time jealously.

Third, get comfortable. Sit in a comfortable chair with legs and arms uncrossed or in some other comfortable place and position. Be comfortable but not in a position where you are likely to fall asleep.

Fourth, close your eyes to help you concentrate easier.

Fifth, relax every muscle in your body. Start with your feet. Tense them real tight, hold for a couple of seconds, then consciously let them go loose and relaxed. Move to your calves, thighs, buttocks, tummy, chest, fists and forearms, biceps, shoulders, neck, and then your face-repeating this same pattern. Focusing on each area of the body, tensing it, then letting it go helps take tension away. Doing this even without any kind of mental meditation is relaxing and is a great stress reliever.

Sixth, commit and trust your mind to God asking him to guide you, to protect your mind from harmful thoughts, and to bring to mind any truth you need to see, any issue you need to deal with, or any creative idea he wants you to work on.

Seventh, breathe deeply. This helps your body to relax and relieve tension. It gets more oxygen into the brain which helps get you out of your head and into your inner self. That is, it clears the mind so you can listen to what your heart or inner self is saying. As God said through David, "When you are on your beds, search your hearts and be silent,"[16] or as *The Living Bible* puts it, "Lie quietly upon your bed in silent meditation."

Eighth, Somebody once said, "Prayer is talking; meditation is listening." While praying for the day's needs and direction for your day is important, before you do this, concentrate on just one thought from God's Word and listen to what God might be saying to you from his Word. For example, my meditative thought for today is, "The Lord is good, a refuge in times of trouble. He cares for those who trust in him."[17] The more I concentrate on this or a similar thought (especially from the Psalms), the greater sense of peace it gives me, not only during times of meditation but during times when I am going through rough waters.

Ninth, music. The important thing regarding meditation is to find a method that works for you. Personally speaking I don't find meditation easy. I have so many things I like to do besides coping with the everyday pressures of too many responsibilities. In younger days I used to play guitar. I hadn't played in many years but have picked it up again as I find it helps get my mind off my work and to meditate musically. I admit that I hate twang-bang-twang guitar "music" so I play melody with chords and sing very softly (just to myself and God) some of the old time hymns I grew up with as well as some of the more contemporary praise choruses. I like to play songs that come from my heart that help me worship and praise God, as well as songs that are petitions to God such as the hymn penned by Robert Robinson.

Oh to grace how great a debtor
Daily I'm constrained to be!
Let thy grace, Lord, like a fetter,
Bind my wandering heart to Thee:
Prone to wander, Lord, I feel it,
Prone to leave the God I love:
Take my heart, O, take and seal it,
Seal it for thy courts above.

Many of the old choruses as well as the contemporary praise songs can be very helpful and inspirational too. Songs such as, "I Surrender All," "Jesus Is the Sweetest Name I Know," "Majesty," "Oh Lord, You're Beautiful," "Refiner's Fire," and many more. As Paul admonished the early Christians saying, "Speaking to yourselves in psalms and hymns and spiritual songs, singing and making melody in your heart to the Lord."[18]

A word of caution

A word of caution, however: if some idea or "word" comes to you that is contrary to or not in harmony with the Scriptures, then you can be sure that it is not from God and needs to be dismissed. Words, thoughts, ideas that pop into our head can come from any number of places. They can come from our unconscious mind, from an association with some other idea, from things that are happening around us, from one's fantasy life, from somebody else's suggestion, or from a score of sources other than from God. Some, too, can come from the tempter.

The following doesn't have to do with meditation but the principle is the same. Recently I heard a prominent preacher on TV, who was raising support, tell viewers that the amount of money that just popped into their heads was what God wanted them to give. Yeah. Right! I think not.

Whether it is how much money we give or any other decision of significance, we need to seek God's guidance in thoughtful prayer and wise consideration. To suggest that the amount of money that just popped into their head is God telling them what they should give can be a powerful way to manipulate sincere Christians to give to the announcer's particular cause! God has given us a heart, true, and he expects us to use it. He has also given us a head and expects us to use that too. Both need to be used together and in harmony with God's thoughts as found in his Word.

I recall one occasion when I was involved in organizing a weekend of meetings for a man raising funds for what seemed like a very worthwhile Christian cause. After the first night I left my wallet at home. The man was a master manipulator and there was no way that I was going to "give to the Lord" out of false guilt being used by a high-pressured manipulating preacher. If I gave for that reason, I would not be a cheerful giver and afterwards would be very angry feeling that I'd been duped.

Any word or idea that comes during times of meditation (or when listening to high-powered preachers) needs to be tested for its validity, the major test being, is it in harmony with the Scriptures? We also need to be wary of the enemy, "for Satan himself masquerades as an angel of light."[19]

Meditation moments

Besides disciplining ourselves to have a daily quiet time to read from the Scriptures and meditating on a thought from what we read, with practice we can learn to shut our mind off from the pressures of the moment and have a minute meditation or two throughout the day.

Take a moment here and there to imagine or picture being in a setting of peace such as walking along a quiet beach either alone or walking with Jesus. Or visually see yourself being in any quiet, peaceful place. See yourself as being calm and relaxed, healthy and well. Or imagine the Lord being your Shepherd leading you through green pastures beside still waters and restoring your soul. Practice seeing in your mind's eye every day what you believe God wants you to be and do. Do this in the morning when you first awake, the last thing at night before you go to sleep, and in quiet moments throughout the day.

The Master Physician said, "Come to me, all you who are weary and burdened, and I will give you rest. Take my yoke upon you and learn from me, for I am gentle and humble in heart, and you will find rest for your souls."[20] And three thousand years ago God, through Solomon, said, "A cheerful heart is good medicine, but a crushed spirit dries up the bones."[21]

Relaxation and creative meditation are not a cure-all for all our stresses and ills, but they can certainly help towards achieving both a restful soul and a cheerful heart—both essential for total well-being—physically, emotionally, and spiritually.

Footnotes:

1. Joan Borysenko, Ph.D., Minding the Body, Mending the Mind (New York, Bantam Books, 1987), 2.
2. Ibid, 2.
3. Psalm 1:1-3, (NIV).
4. Proverbs 14:30, (NIV) and (TLB).
5. Mark 7:31.
6. Psalm 46:10, (NIV).
7. Exodus 23:1.
8. Isaiah 14:12, (NIV).
9. Isaiah 14:13-15, (NIV).
10. Joshua 1:7-9, (NIV).
11. Psalm 1:1-2.
12. Psalm 119:11.
13. Psalm 23:1-3, (NIV).
14. Psalm 56:11, (NIV).
15. Proverbs 14:30.
16. Psalm 4:4, (NIV).
17. Nahum 1:7, (NIV).
18. Ephesians 5:19.
19. 2 Corinthians 11:14, (NIV).
20. Matthew 11:28-29, (NIV).
21. Proverbs 17:22, (NIV).

"For many people, religion
is as much an addiction as
alcoholism, smoking, problem
gambling, and work addiction."

12

What You Do Is What You Get

"MY NAME IS LEO. I am an alcoholic, a codependent, a religious addict and a religious abuser. I am a recovering priest."[1] This is how the Reverend Leo Booth, an Episcopal priest introduces himself.

Leo is a recovering alcoholic and, at the time, had been sober for fourteen years. He also pointed out that he was recovering from a very narrow-minded religion.

Booth, author of the book, *When God Becomes a Drug*, explains how that for many people, religion is as much an addiction as alcoholism, smoking, problem gambling, and work addiction. He states that religious addiction is just as big a problem as alcohol addiction because the abuser wants God or Jesus to fix his life, to take away his problems and his pain without accepting personal responsibility for them.

In other words, God helps those who help themselves. True, God is on our side, but we also need to accept responsibility for our thinking and our behavior.

Far too many addicts expect God to deliver them with little or no effort on their part. I've witnessed abused women who believe they have to stay in their situation in obedience to God, and keep praying for God to deliver them without doing the necessary footwork themselves.

Leo Booth spent years asking God to help him overcome his problem and to give him the strength to resist the temptation to keep drinking without his putting the cork in the bottle—or getting rid of the bottle. And the more he drank the more he escaped into religion, and the more extreme he became in his religious practices in order to medicate his guilt and pain with ritual and dogma.

Religious addiction can be just as destructive to the family as any other addiction because the addict is in denial and isn't facing his real problems nor accepting responsibility for his recovery. Instead, the person needs to face his problems and get into recovery.

Religious addicts seek to escape from reality, but Jesus told us to be responsible and to confront our problems head on, which brings us to our next law for healing and wholeness: the law of wholesome living.

Law seven: The law of wholesome living

Expecting God to heal our sicknesses when we fail to clean up our act and live according to the principles spelled out in his instruction book, the Bible, is about as realistic as expecting our car to keep on running if we never change the oil, don't get it serviced regularly, put junk fuel in the gas tank, and neglect to keep the tires inflated.

Dr. William Saddler said, "No one can appreciate so fully as a doctor the amazingly large percentage of human disease and suffering which is directly traceable to worry, fear, conflict, immorality, dissipation, and ignorance—to unwholesome thinking and unclean living. The sincere acceptance of the principles and teachings of Christ with respect to the life of mental peace and joy, the life of unselfish thought and clean living, would at once wipe out more than half the difficulties, diseases, and sorrows of the human race. In other words, more than one half of the present affliction of mankind could be prevented by the tremendous prophylactic power of actually living up to the personal and practical spirit of the real teachings of Christ."[2]

Easier said than done

But as most of us have found, cleaning up our act and living by the good book is much easier said than done.

I recall one of my teachers in Bible school instructing us that the best way to break a bad habit was to drop it. A clever pun, but unfortunately, overcoming bad habits and resolving life's problems isn't that simple. As already emphasized, most acting out in negative and self-destructive behaviors are symptoms of deeper problems—the fruit of deeper roots.

If an individual's bad habit is nothing more than a bad habit and isn't a symptom of a deeper problem, then dropping it may be all that is needed. If, on the other hand, an alcoholic who has an addictive personality, stops drinking but doesn't resolve the cause of his addiction, he, like Leo Booth, will attach his addictive issue to something else like religion, work, sex, food, or any one of a number of other self-destructive habits or behaviors and act it out in that way.

This, of course, is not an excuse to keep acting out. Not at all. We need to stop acting out (stop the addictive behavior), not as the means to overcome the destructive behavior, but to stop medicating or anesthetizing the pain that is the root cause driving the addictive and/or negative behaviors. Only as we face, feel, confront, and resolve the real pain and bring it to the light can we seek and find God's healing.

Wholesome living is critical for spiritual, emotional and spiritual health, but, as Leo Booth also pointed out, the key to make this possible is to get into recovery. That is, we need to actively participate in a program that helps us to confront the root cause/s of our problems and sicknesses, work through and resolve these so we can find physical, emotional, relational, and spiritual healing and overcome the difficulties we are having.

The power of relationships

As a general rule, most, if not all recovery and healing, takes place in healing relationships. Fundamentally, we were wounded in damaging relationships and often get sick because of sick relationships. Subsequently, we are made whole in wholesome relationships and healthy in healing relationships. Healthy, healing relationships are where one feels safe to bring all of his problems to the light and still be loved and accepted as he or she is. It is this loving acceptance that begins the process of healing.

At the core of negative, self-destructive behavior is that we don't feel loved, accepted, and affirmed at the very core of our being. Thus, to overcome negative behavior and be truly healed physically, emotionally, and spiritually, we need to feel loved and affirmed at the very core of our being by others —and by God. As St. Augustine of Hippo so insightfully said, "You have made us for yourself, O Lord, and our hearts are restless until they find their rest in you."

Love is a feeling to be learned

Love, however, is something we learn. We don't come into

the world knowing how to love, only with the capacity to love. We learn it by example. As the Apostle John wrote, "We love God because he first loved us."[3] We learn to love people in exactly the same way. If we didn't receive sufficient love when growing up, we will obviously have a love deficiency as adults and what we didn't get back then we need to get now.

As we pointed out in an earlier chapter, we don't learn to love by loving others. We may grow in love by doing this, but first we need to learn by somebody first loving us unconditionally. If we never received this love when we were growing up, we need to receive it now because it is foundational for healing and recovery. The way we receive this love is to be in a safe, non-judgmental, accepting and affirming relationship with at least one other person, and preferably several with whom we feel safe to allow them to see and know us as we are—warts and all.

For some of us it may require one-on-one counseling with a competent, trained counselor. For others it may mean to be in a twelve-step or similar recovery group. Or it may need to be as a member of a committed small support group where we feel safe to be open and honest and deal with gut-level issues—not just sit around and talk off the top of our heads about our symptoms, and never get into gut level feelings to deal with the root causes of the difficulties we are struggling with

To love is to risk

To open up is to become vulnerable and is risky business to be sure. However, not to open up and be vulnerable is an even greater risk for without access to our truth and bringing it to the light, there is no healing or recovery.

In healing relationships, as I open up and allow you to see my total self—my strengths, weaknesses, sins, failures, hurts, anger, guilt, shame, and my total dark side—and you love, accept and affirm me—little by little I learn to love and accept myself and begin to feel affirmed at the core of my being. This is foundational for learning to love and accept myself in a healthy way, and in turn, helping me to love and accept others in a healthy way, and also for learning to feel God's love and his affirmation at the very core of my being—which, in turn, is foundational for physical, emotional, relational, and spiritual healing and for overcoming self-destructive behaviors.

When Jesus told us to love our neighbor as ourselves, he was affirming that he wants us to love ourselves. If we hate ourselves and are filled with shame, we cannot be loving towards others. As Leo Booth put it, "Shamed-based thinking reinforces the belief that you don't make mistakes, but that you are the mistake."[4] This in turn leads to addictive behaviors and considerable unhappiness.

King Solomon said, "A joyful heart is good medicine but a broken spirit dries the bones."[5] And again, "Do not forget my teaching, keep my commands in your heart, for they will lengthen your life many years.... Do not let love and truth leave you ... trust the Lord, and turn from evil. This will bring healing to your body, and refreshment to your bones."[6]

A blend of grace, truth, and love is the key to overcoming negative behaviors and the healing of the whole person.

Following the law of wholesome living is the law of discipline and determination.

Law 8: the law of discipline and determination

Achieving anything worthwhile takes strong desire, the decision to do what we need to do to make it happen, and the discipline and determination to keep on doing it for the long haul.

Unfortunately, for many people discipline often doesn't

last. One reason is because discipline without feeling loved and affirmed is like putting a Band-Aid over an abscess without draining the poison. And while desire, decision, discipline, and determination are all needed for achieving and maintaining total well-being, it is important to follow all other laws for healing, otherwise discipline will go the way of all other good intentions—out the window.

The person, for example, who overeats often has an empty love tank and tries to fill it with food. Telling this person to discipline himself not to overeat without showing him or her how to get their love needs met is worse than useless, as they start out with great intentions but soon fizzle out. The discipline of a healthy diet, as needy as this is, still doesn't meet their true need—they still feel empty so go on a binge and overeat again, then feel defeated, guilty, and a failure. They confess this, go back on their diet, feel empty, overeat ... and the vicious cycle continues.

The law of discipline is essential for wholesome living but we need to put first things first. That is, we need discipline and determination to first resolve the root causes of our ills, get our basic needs for love met in healthy ways, and then apply discipline to other areas of living.

In other words, discipline without love leads to disaster. At the same time, taking care of our love needs first doesn't necessarily make discipline easy, but it does make it more realistic and possible.

Benefits of disciplined living

In their book, *LifeStyle 2000*, Mark and Ernestine Finley report, "After conducting extensive research, Dr. Lester Breslow, Dean of the School of Health at the University of California at Los Angeles, made a startling assertion: 'It is possible, by following seven basic health guidelines [disciplines], to increase American life expectancy by eleven years.'

"Let's look at these seven principles:
- Avoid tobacco
- Limit the use of alcohol. Many researchers feel we would do well to eliminate alcohol altogether.
- Avoid eating between meals.
- Get adequate rest (seven to eight hours per night).
- Engage in frequent exercise.
- Remain close to your ideal weight.
- Eat a good breakfast every day."[7]

Start the day right

According to the Finleys and other health specialists, breakfast is the most important meal of the day. They quote an old saying that says, "Eat breakfast like a king, lunch like a prince, and supper like a pauper."[8] The reason being that we need fuel for the day's work and activities, not at the evening meal for the night's rest.

"A number of years ago, the United States Government studied thousands of children in the state of Iowa in an attempt to evaluate whether eating a good breakfast made any difference in their classroom attitudes, their ability to learn, and their all-around performance. These massive studies indicated the detrimental effect of skipping breakfast and the positive benefits of eating a good breakfast....

"Among the detrimental effects of skipping breakfast was a lowered attention span as well as poorer classroom attitudes. Those students who skipped breakfast tended to be much more fidgety and anxious; they were prone to be significantly more restless, and their general attitudes and thoughts tended to be much poorer. Among the beneficial effects of eating a good breakfast were: increased attention span, positive classroom attitudes, and a greater learning ability (memory)."[9]

Eat right to be right

Not only is eating right at breakfast time important but maintaining a healthy high fiber, low fat, well-balanced diet (without being fanatical and compulsive), and total care of the body are also essential for maintaining a healthy body and mind.

It is useless to expect the medics, God, or anybody else to heal us if we don't exercise the discipline of taking proper care of our bodies. For instance, such a simple thing as drinking more than three cups of coffee a day, according to one doctor, "may predispose you to a coronary heart attack and even moderate amounts of coffee can cause irritability."[10]

Sweet sickness

Insufficient physical exercise, an overload of unresolved stress, high blood cholesterol, high blood pressure, being overweight ("if you can pinch an inch, it's too much"), cigarette smoking, and insufficient rest also add to the predisposition for a heart attack even more in a man than in a woman.[11] Also, eating too much sugar "appears to be a contributing factor to coronary heart disease, particularly when combined with a high-fat diet."[12]

Furthermore, eating too much sugar can be detrimental to other areas of health, and the average American diet is overloaded with it. According to the Finleys the average American eats twenty times the amount of sugar today as he did in the early 1800s. Cookies, cakes, ice-cream, candy, soft drinks are all loaded with sugar. "One piece of chewing gum has a half teaspoon of sugar, a glazed donut—six teaspoons, three scoops of ice cream—twelve teaspoons, a banana split—twenty-four teaspoons of sugar. Every piece of candy is seventy-five to eighty percent sugar."[13]

The highly respected Loma Linda University in Loma Linda, California, "has done some significant research on sugar and its relationship to disease. The researchers have discovered that there is a significant temporary decrease in the ability of certain white blood cells, the phagocytes, to destroy bacteria after a person eats a large amount of sugar at one time.

"Normal levels of white blood cell activity do not return until five to six hours later.... It's astounding to recognize that there is a major reduction in the ability of the body to fight off disease. This is why children who eat a lot of sweets are particularly vulnerable to colds and infections."[14]

For additional information on healthy living I recommend the reading of the Finley's book, *LifeStyle 2000*. It can be ordered from your local bookstore or from the publisher, Creation Enterprises International, P.O. Box 274, Siloam Springs, Arkansas 72761.

In summary, for a wholesome and disciplined lifestyle the Finleys suggest the following "Eight Secrets to Better Health":

- Eat a well-balanced natural diet.
- Strive to exercise daily. (Consult your physician for details.)
- Use plenty of pure water (drink six to eight glasses per day).
- Bathe daily.
- Soak up some sunlight every day.
- Avoid unhealthy items such as alcohol, tobacco, and drugs.
- Breathe plenty of pure air daily.
- Be sure to get proper rest (eight hours on the average per day).
- Be thankful and trust in God who made you and loves to care for you."[15]

As well as wholesome living, loving relationships, and disciplined living, there are two more laws that are vital for healing of the whole person. These are the law of prayer and the law of belief, which we will address in the next and final chapter.

Footnotes:

1. Leo Booth, *When God Becomes a Drug* (Los Angeles, California, Jeremy P.Tarcher, Inc., 1991), 1.
2. S.I. McMillen, *None of These Diseases* (Westwood, New Jersey, Spire Books, Fleming H. Revell Company, 1963), 67.
3. 1 John 4:9.
4. Leo Booth, *When God Becomes a Drug*, 62.
5. Proverbs 17:22.
6. Proverbs 8:1-8.
7. Mark and Ernestine Finley, *LifeStyle 2000*, (Siloam Springs, Arkansas: Creation Enterprises International, 1993), 12-13.
8. Ibid, 13.
9. Ibid, 14.
10. Ibid, 33.
11. Ibid, 32-33.
12. Ibid, 60.
13. Ibid, 57-58.
14. Ibid, 62.
15. Ibid, 91.

*Do not forget my teaching,
keep my commands in your
heart, for they will lengthen your
life many years ... Do not let love
and truth leave you ... trust the Lord,
and turn from evil. This will bring
health to your body, and
refreshment to your bones.*

– Proverbs 3:1 (NIV)

13

According to Your Faith

AN OVERCAST SKY made the country night intensely dark and a light drizzle made the highway dangerously slick. On my way home that night as I passed a semi-trailer and pulled back in front of it, my car struck a slippery patch of roadway and went slithering snake-like down the road—totally out of my control. The next thing I knew my car swung around and began careening down the road backwards with the semi-trailer barreling down on top of me!

In terror I prayed, "God, help!"

With only moments to spare, my car suddenly flipped sideways out of the path of the oncoming semi and went skidding sideways off the highway and down an embankment. Certain that my car would now overturn, in terror, I prayed again, "Help, God!"

Amazingly, my car didn't overturn, but neither did it stop. It swung around and then went bouncing forward through bushes and brush alongside the highway. "Oh, no,"

I thought, "now I'll end up smashing into a tree."

Again I prayed, "Help, God!"

Eventually my car stopped in front of some bushes. Miraculously I missed every post by the roadside and every tree in the field, backed up a few feet and drove very nervously back onto the freeway and on my way home without a single bruise to myself or a scratch on my car. Prayer—earnest prayer—is very powerful which brings us to another law for healing: The law of prayer.

Law nine: The law of prayer

Was my protection in what could have easily been a fatal highway accident a coincidence, or does God answer prayer and help us when we call on him, not only in times of emergency, but also when we pray for healing and other needs in everyday life?

In my experience I have found that God does answer prayer—sometimes quickly; sometimes slowly. Some prayers don't get answered, at least the way I want them to. Others seem like they haven't risen beyond the ceiling.

Effective prayer, however, isn't turning to God only in times of need, nor is it a lucky charm to win special favors. Neither is God or prayer a painkiller as John Powell put it—like a giant Bayer's aspirin: "Take God three times a day and you won't feel any pain!"[1] Such prayers are not effective, but genuine prayer is—even if God's answer is sometimes "No."

As a jokester once said about how God answers prayer: Sometimes he says, "Yes." Sometimes he says, "No." And sometimes he says, "You've got to be kidding." Reading between the lines, there's a lot of truth in that insight.

Seriously however, the key to all effective prayer is learning to pray the right prayer. As the Bible says, "You do not have, because you do not ask God. And when you do ask, you don't receive because you ask wrongly—with wrong motives—for selfish reasons."[2]

How then do we pray the right prayer?

❏ First, pray responsibly

Asking God to do for us what we can and need to do for ourselves is irresponsible and immature. Many a time, for example, in student days, I'd pray furiously for God's help at examination time—especially when I wasn't adequately prepared. I managed to pass all of my exams, but certainly not because of my pray-at-the-last-moment-instead-of-study prayers.

It is true that God's Word says, "Is any one of you in trouble? He should pray. Is anyone happy? Let him sing songs of praise. Is any one of you sick? He should call the elders of the church to pray over him and anoint him with oil in the name of the Lord. And the prayer offered in faith will make the sick person well; the Lord will raise him up. If he has sinned, he will be forgiven."[3] But that is not all there is to it ... it's only a part of the answer for the rest of the "law" for healing (as we have emphasized in an earlier chapter) is found in the next verse, "Therefore confess your sins to each other and pray for each other so that you may be healed. The prayer of a righteous man is powerful and effective,"[4] which shows what our responsibility is in the healing process.

❏ Second, pray realistically

When we have a problem, a habit that has us beaten, a personal conflict, or some sickness, we tend to focus our prayer on the symptom rather than on the cause. As counselor Dr. Cecil Osborne explained, "When we unconsciously cover a deeper sin or fault, we tend to confess a lesser one all the more vigorously." How true this is. This is because we are afraid to face the real problem behind the presenting problem.

In every problem, conflict, and/or sickness I may experience, before praying for healing, I need to ask God to give me the insight and courage to see and face any possible cause/s behind my problem or sickness, the willingness to admit what I might be contributing to it, and the courage and determination (with God's help) to do what I need to do to resolve it.

❏ *Third, pray honestly*

If I pray that God will bless my neighbor but in my heart I hate him, which prayer will God hear? Obviously, what my heart is saying. The only way God will bless my neighbor in answer to my prayer is if I admit that I hate him and ask God to help me to love him.

Rote prayers, meaningless repetition, verbosity, or prayers from the top of the head don't mean a thing to God.[5] The prayers he hears and answers are the honest ones that come from the heart. As the psalmist wrote, "The Lord is near to all who call on him, to all who call on him in truth."[6]

To "call on God in truth" means to be perfectly honest with myself and God, keeping in mind that if I am not honest with myself, there's no way I can be honest with God. Thus to find healing I need to see, admit, confess and confront the truth—that is, the root cause/s of my problems.

Speaking personally, whenever I have a symptom—be it physical, emotional, relational, or spiritual—I always ask God to reveal to me the truth behind the particular problem. I also tell God that I am willing to be made willing to see it no matter how painful it may be, because, for me, it usually takes pain to break through my defenses that I have built up to avoid facing my inner truth. That is; it's only when my pain is greater than my fear that I am ready to see the truth.

Sometimes I add a doubtful P.S. to this prayer, asking God that if possible, to please do it gently! I think God just smiles and says, "Silly boy. You know better than that." God has already told us what it takes to learn patience. Overcoming most problems also takes tribulation and pain.

Keep in mind, too, that if all we do is focus our prayer on the symptom (the presenting problem) and ask God to heal us of that, all we do is reinforce the problem. Doing so is praying the wrong prayer. Praying the right prayer is not to neglect the symptom, but to focus our prayer on the root cause/s behind the symptom and asking God to heal us of that.

❏ *Fourth, pray specifically*

Recently I had an equipment need for my work and prayed that God would show me how to get the funds for this need this month! I woke up in the middle of that night and, being unable to go back to sleep, got up and worked on balancing my finances. To my amazement I found a mistake in my favor and was able to order the equipment the next day!

Many people say that God answers our prayers according to his timing. Perhaps, just perhaps, it may have more to do with our timing—when we are willing and able to handle the truth. A simple prayer such as the one in the previous illustration regarding the equipment I needed doesn't really have any hidden cause that blocks God's answer—unless if one is praying with a wrong motive. But when it comes to the healing of the whole person, there can be very complex causes and deep fears that need to be faced and dealt with before we see the final result of our healing. Praying for a piece of equipment is more an event. Praying for the healing of the whole person is a process, a process that can take a lot of hard work, pain, and time. The principles for healing may be simple to understand but not easy to put into practice.

❏ *Fifth, pray persistently*

Not all my prayers get answered as quickly as praying for

a piece of needed equipment. I wish they did, but some things I had prayed for for years before I received the answer.

If our prayer is legitimate, sometimes we need to be as persistent as Jacob who once said to God, "I will not let you go until you bless me."[8] Jesus himself said, "Ask and it will be given to you; seek and you will find; knock and the door will be opened to you. For everyone who asks receives; he who seeks finds; and to him who knocks, the door will be opened."[9] The implication is to keep on asking, seeking, and knocking until you receive that for which you are praying. These words of Jesus also imply that receiving an answer to some prayers is a process and not just a quick fix or a simple event.

❏ *Sixth, pray in harmony with God's will*

The Bible says, "If we ask anything according to God's will, he hears us. And if we know that he hears us in whatever we ask, we know that we have the request which we have asked from him."[10]

High on God's priorities for us is our growth and maturity. Prayers in harmony with this principle will always be effective.

Pardon the poor grammar, but in my own experience whenever I have prayed according to this principle and for truth, I have never not received an answer to these prayers.

❏ *Seventh, pray sincerely*

"Do you want to get well?"[11] was Jesus' approach. In other words, if we want God to answer our prayers, we need to want the answer bad enough that we are willing to pay the price. For instance, if we want to grow in faith, love, patience, perseverance, and maturity, we need to realize that all of these are learned through experience, often painful experiences. As the Bible says, "Tribulation works patience— suffering produces perseverance."[12]

❑ *Finally, come to God on his terms*

Most important of all, effective prayer is dependent on our having a right relationship with God through his Son, Jesus Christ. He is the only way to God and the only one through whom we can approach God. "Nobody can come to God except through me,"[13] Jesus said. Because of our sin, our relationship with God has been severed. But because of Christ's death for us on the cross, our relationship with God can be restored by our accepting Jesus Christ into our heart and life as personal Lord and Savior and then coming to God through him.

When we are living in a right relationship with God, and learn to pray the right prayers, we can be certain that God will answer them. As Jesus put it, "If you stay in me [in right relationship with me] and obey my commands, you may ask any request you like and it will be granted!"[14]

Last but not least, we come to the "tenth commandment" for healing and wholeness which is the law of belief.

Law ten: The law of belief

It should go without saying that prayer without faith is like going sailing and not hoisting your sail. Faith is not only essential for effective prayer, but also for all phases of healing, growth, and recovery.

❑ *First, faith in God*

"Without faith it is impossible to please God, because anyone who comes to him must believe that he exists and that he rewards those who earnestly seek him."[15]

Jesus himself said, "All things, whatever you ask in

193

prayer, believing, you will receive."[16] And to the two blind men who came to him wanting to be healed, Jesus "asked them, 'Do you believe that I am able to do this?'

"'Yes, Lord,' they replied.

"Then he touched their eyes and said, 'According to your faith will it be done to you'; and their sight was restored."[17]

As Jesus said, "Therefore I tell you, whatever you ask for in prayer, believe that you have received it, and it will be yours. And when you stand praying, if you hold anything against anyone, forgive him, so that your Father in heaven may forgive you your sins."[18]

❏ *Second, faith that God's blessings are available for us*

Sometimes it is much easier to believe that healing and answers to prayer are available to others, but not to us. The reality is, they are as much available to us—you and me—as they are to anyone else. God or life doesn't have favorites. Unless we believe they are available for us, we will never go after them.

It has been said before that we don't always live the life we profess but we always live the life we believe. If we believe we are a failure, we will set ourselves up to fail. If we believe we are bad we will act badly. If we believe we are unlovable, we will act in an unlovable manner and set people up to reject us. If we don't believe God answers our prayers, he won't. If we don't believe he will heal us, he won't. And if we don't believe growth and healing are possible for us, they won't be. Our lack of faith blocks the answers, not God.

On the other hand, if we believe, we will receive. Jesus not only said that things would happen to us according to our faith, but also, "All things are possible for him who believes."[19]

I agree with Norman Cousins, author of *Anatomy of an Illness*, who said when it comes to physical healing, "Drugs are not always necessary. Belief in recovery always is."[20] It's not enough to profess or say we believe—we need to truly believe and act accordingly.

194

❏ *Third, faith in ourselves*

We need faith not only in God and that his blessings are available to us, but also faith in ourselves. This is not a conceited or prideful belief in our own omnipotence. Not at all. It is a solid belief that what we need to do for ourselves, and do, will be effective.

A man by the name of Baudjuin once said, "To be ambitious for wealth, and yet always expecting to be poor; to be always doubting your ability to get what you long for, is like trying to reach east by traveling west. There is no philosophy which will help man to succeed when he is always doubting his ability to do so, and thus attracting failure. No matter how hard you work for success if your thought is saturated with the fear of failure, it will kill your efforts, neutralize your endeavors and make success impossible."[21]

Jesus also said, "I tell you the truth, if anyone says to this mountain, 'Go, throw yourself into the sea,' and does not doubt in his heart but believes that what he says will happen, it will be done for him."[22]

Only those who believe that with God's help they can remove the mountains that block their healing, and do what they need to do to make it happen, can and will remove those mountains. Faith, that is applied faith and not wishful thinking, does remove mountains. Or as James put it, "Faith without works is dead."[23]

❏ *Miracles, not magic*

When it comes to healing, whether physical, emotional or spiritual, or overcoming other difficulties, in some cases God gives quick answers to prayer. Mostly, however, if we are to follow God's principles for healing and recovery, we need to remember that healing is primarily a process rather than a single event. Again, if the cause of my illness or problem is within myself, of which my suffering is a symptom, it is naive of me to expect God to take away my symptoms if I refuse to face and deal with the causes. God will not do this. As Dr. Cecil Osborne says, "Only the immature, the childish expect instantaneous, miraculous answers to life's problems."

All healing and recovery, whether fast or slow, is still a miracle. When people look for instant healing for physical ills, and/or a quick fix to resolve their personal problems without accepting responsibility for their recovery, they are confusing miracles for magic. Yes, I believe in miracles but not magic. Miracles usually take much longer!

When we deal with the issues in our life that make us sick and cause our problems, we clear the way for God to heal us. For instance, if I have a cut that is infected it will need to be lanced to drain away the yucky puss so that healing antiseptic can be applied to make healing possible. This may be very painful but very essential. When I have supercharged repressed negative emotions such as hurt, resentment, an unforgiving spirit and so on, they, like the puss in an infected sore, also need to be drained away so that healing and recovery can happen. It may be crude but I repeat, repressed negative emotions give us "emotional constipation" and poison our entire system—physically, emotionally, relationally, and spiritually.

God doesn't drain the poison of this pain. That's our responsibility. "Get rid of it," God says. Repressing and denying it doesn't get rid of it. That allows the infection to worsen. We need to want healing bad enough that we are willing to accept full responsibility to do our part in the healing process. When we do it God's way, healing, growth, and recovery happen. This we need to believe and act upon in faith.

A final word

As all ten laws or "principles" for healing are an integral part of God's formula for the healing of body, mind, and spirit, adhering to any one law can bring a measure of healing in and of itself—depending on the nature and cause of the illness or problem.

Adhering to several of these laws can bring an even greater measure of healing even if one never prays or doesn't believe in God. God's laws work whether we believe in him or not (e.g. the law of gravity). However, believing God and adhering faithfully to all "ten laws" for healing and wholeness will guarantee recovery from many, if not most, of life's conflicts and for many sicknesses where the cause/s lie within ourselves—and where we accept responsibility for facing these causes and doing our part in resolving them.

One may have cancer, as a friend of mind did, and claim to be cured by prayer, which my friend did. He believed he was healed and for a year appeared to be. However, what he interpreted as faith was actually living in denial. The root of his cancer and any underlying possible causes were never considered, confronted, or dealt with. And all the while the cancer within kept growing. A year later the cancer got my friend. He died in the prime of life.

Life's like that. Whatever our "cancer" may be—whether it is physical, emotional, moral, and/or spiritual—we either get the cancer or the cancer gets us. We either get (resolve) the root cause/s of our ills and conflicts caused by stress, bitterness, resentment, an unforgiving spirit, envy, jealousy, guilt and so on, or these "cancerous" issues get us. The choice is ours.

God has given us a plan for healing, wholeness, peace, contentment, and creative living. We can't improve on his plan. The best and wisest thing to do is to get in on it. Beware of quick fixes that offer easy solutions and promise instant success but avoid God's plan. Salvation is a process. Growth and maturity are a process. Recovery is a process and much of healing is a process. The fakes and the phonies may seemingly produce some quick results, but in the long run, they can't produce lasting results. Only God's way can do that.

As Jesus said, "Don't worry about things—food, drink, and clothes. Don't be anxious about tomorrow. God will take care of your tomorrow too. Live one day at a time."[24] A thousand years earlier, God through Solomon said, "Do not forget my teaching, keep my commands in your heart, for they will lengthen your life many years ... Do not let love and truth leave you ... trust the Lord, and turn from evil. This will bring health to your body, and refreshment to your bones."[25]

Grace, truth, and love combined are the key to healing, wholeness, growth, and contentment. Grace is needed for truth to be revealed, love is the healing agent, and the truth sets us free; that is, if we adhere to it.

As Jesus said to the Jews who believed Him, "If you abide in My word, you are My disciples indeed. And you shall know the truth, and the truth shall make you free."[26]

When we do healing God's way, our broken wing will be healed and we will learn to fly again. As God's Word says:

"Even youths grow tired and weary,
and young men stumble and fall;
but those who hope in the LORD
will renew their strength.
They will soar on wings like eagles;
they will run and not grow weary,
they will walk and not be faint"[27]

Footnotes:

1. John Powell, *Why Am I Afraid to Love* (Chicago: Argus Communications Co., 1967), 34.

2. James 4:2-3, (Paraphrase).
3. James 5:13-15, (NIV).
4. James 5:16, (NIV).
5. Matthew 6:7.
6. Psalm 145:18, (NIV).
7. Romans 5:3.
8. Genesis 32:26, (TLB).
9. Matthew 7:7-8, (NIV).
10. 1 John 5:14-15, (NIV).
11. John 5:6, (NIV).
13. Romans 5:3, (KJV) and (NIV).
13. John 14:6.
14. John 15:7, (TLB).
15. Hebrews 11:6, (NIV).
16. Matthew 21:22, (NIV).
17. Matthew 9:28-30, (NIV).
18. Mark 11:24-25, (NIV).
19. Mark 9:23.
20. Norman Cousins, *Anatomy of an Illness as Perceived by the Patient*, (New York, NY: Bantam Books, Inc., 1981), 50.
21. Baudjuin, quoted in a sermon by Dick Innes in Lansing, Michigan, 1966.
22. Mark 11:23, (NIV).
23. James 2:20.
24. Matthew 6:25, 4, (T;B).
25. Proverbs 3:1-3, 7-8.
26. John 8:31-32, (NKJV).
27. Isaiah 40:30-31, (NIV).

Epilogue

For articles by Dick Innes on personal and spiritual growth visit www.actsweb.org, the web site of ACTS International. To receive his *Daily Encounter* (without charge)—the popular weekday e-mail devotional—go to www.actsweb.org/detoday. To purchase other helpful materials by Dick go to www.actscom.com/store.

ACTS International, founded by Dick Innes, is a non-profit church service organization whose purpose is to help bridge the gap between the church and the non-church community. This is achieved through literature, life-enrichment seminars, e-mail, and the Internet.

Based on the words of Jesus, "Do you want to be made whole?" ACTS goal is to apply the gospel and Christian message to the healing of the whole person and thereby help people become healthier spiritually, physically, and emotionally and thereby greatly enhance their relationships.

We believe that God is not so much concerned about religion as he is about relationships. That is, he not only wants us to have a right relationship with him through Jesus Christ, but also with each other and ourselves. We also believe that God's goal is not to make people good simply for goodness sake, but to make people whole; for only to the degree that we are made whole will our lifestyle, actions, attitudes, behavior, health, and relationships be wholesome.

To learn more about ACTS International visit the ACTS website at www.actsweb.org or contact one of the following offices:

U.S.A
Richard (Dick) Innes, Director
ACTS International
PO Box 73545
San Clemente, CA 92673-0119
U.S.A.
Telephone: 1-949-940-9050
Fax: 1-949-481-3686
E-Mail: acts@actsweb.org
Web: www.actsweb.org
www.actscom.com/store

Australia
Terry George, Managing Director
ACTS International
PO Box 88
Kent Town, SA 5071
Australia
Telephone: 08-8336-8866
Fax: 08-8336-8877
E-mail: actsint@adelaide.on.net
Web: www.actsinternational.org/au

New Zealand
Barrie McClymont, Director
ACTS International
PO Box 45-121
Auckland 1230
New Zealand
Telephone: 09-834-4567
Fax: 09-834-4081
E-mail: ACTS3INC@xtra.co.nz
Web: www.actsinternational.org/nz